' "Leave the dead som̲_____irge-Man in Wole Soyinka's beau̲_____he living are not willing t̲o_____between the desire of the_____ng to avoid it. This confli̲c_____ho leads both to a judgme̲_____his labours will effect any rea̲_____...

'The play o̲p_____two dead ancestors, thrusting their heads up from _____ams. They had been summoned by the living to attend ___ gathering of the tribes" (an analogue of Nigerian Independence?), but instead of being the idealized figures of the tribal imagination they turn out to be full of ancient bitterness and resentment and are shunned by everyone as "obscenities." However, Forest Father selects four of the living and leads them away deep into the forest where, in company with the dead couple, he forces them to confront their true selves and the repetitive pattern of their weaknesses and crimes.' *Times Literary Supplement.*

'The contemporary theater seems to have forgotten that it has its roots in ritual and song, and it is only the rare emergence of a Lorca or a Brecht—or a Wole Soyinka—that recreates an awareness of our deprivation.' *African Forum.*

'His play, *The Road*, presented in London during the Commonwealth Festival last summer, was described by Penelope Gilliatt in *The Observer* as "having done for our napping language what brigand dramatists from Ireland have done for two centuries, booted it awake, rifled its pockets and scattered the loot into the middle of next week." His novel, *The Interpreters*, has been greeted by an American critic as the work of a new James Joyce. Thanks to the Dakar Festival the two companies that he has founded, the 1960 Masks and Orisun Theatre were seen for the first time in full strength outside Nigeria in his play, *Kongi's Harvest*, and *The Road* got the Dakar prize for drama.' *New Society.*

Three Crown Series

Arnold Apple:	Son of Guyana
J. P. Clark:	Three Plays
	Ozidi
J. C. de Graft:	Through a Film Darkly
	Sons and Daughters
R. Sarif Easmon:	Dear Parent and Ogre
Obi Egbuna:	Daughters of the Sun
Mbuyiseni Oswald Mtshali:	Sounds of a Cowhide Drum
Ola Rotimi:	The Gods are not to Blame
Wole Soyinka:	A Dance of the Forests
	The Lion and the Jewel
	Kongi's Harvest
	The Road
D. O. Umobuarie:	Black Justice
J. Wartemberg:	The Corpse's Comedy

Wole Soyinka

A DANCE
of the
FORESTS

---※---

Oxford University Press

Oxford University Press, Walton Street, Oxford OX2 6DP

OXFORD NEW YORK TORONTO
DELHI BOMBAY CALCUTTA MADRAS KARACHI
PETALING JAYA SINGAPORE HONG KONG TOKYO
NAIROBI DAR ES SALAAM CAPE TOWN
MELBOURNE AUCKLAND

and associated companies in
BERLIN IBADAN

Oxford is a trade mark of Oxford University Press

© Oxford University Press 1963

First published 1963
Ninth impression 1989

Cover designed by Taj Ahmed

Printed in Great Britain by
Thomson Litho Ltd, East Kilbride, Scotland

A DANCE OF THE FORESTS was first performed as part of the
Nigerian Independence Celebrations, October 1960.

Production was by the *1960 Masks*, with the following cast:

DEAD WOMAN *Elizabeth Osisioma*	COUNCILLOR *Wole Siyanbola*
DEAD MAN *Taiye Ayorinde*	MATA KHARIBU *Sola Rhodes*
ADENEBI (and HISTORIAN) *Ralph Opara*	POET'S NOVICE } *Tokunbo Odunjo*
	HALF-CHILD
DEMOKE (and COURT POET) *Yemi Lijadu*	ARONI *Adisa Ajetunmobi*
ROLA (and MADAME TORTOISE) *Olga Adeniyi-Jones*	MURETE *Segun Sofowote*
	OGUN *Afolabi Ajayi*
AGBOREKO *Funmilayo Asekun*	FOREST HEAD } *Elow Gabonal*
OLD MAN } *Patrick Ozieh*	(OBANEJI)
PHYSICIAN	ESHUORO *Remi Adeleye*
DIRGE-MAN, SLAVE- } *Femi Euba*	Dancers *The Ezeagu District Dancing Union*
DEALER and CRIER	Other parts *The Company*

Characters

The Guests of Honour
DEAD WOMAN
DEAD MAN

The Town Dwellers
ADENEBI Council Orator
OBANEJI
DEMOKE A Carver
ROLA A Courtesan
AGBOREKO Elder of Sealed Lips
OLD MAN A Council Elder (father of Demoke)
A DIRGE-MAN
HIS ACOLYTE
COUNCILLORS
BEATERS
DRUMMERS

The Forest Dwellers
ARONI the Lame One
MURETE tree-imp
ESHUORO a wayward cult-spirit
OGUN patron god of carvers
FOREST HEAD masquerading as Obaneji
FOREST CRIER
THE QUESTIONER
THE INTERPRETER
JESTER to Eshuoro
THE TRIPLETS
THE HALF-CHILD
THE ANTS
SPIRITS of the PALM, DARKNESS, RIVERS, etc.

The Court of MATA KHARIBU
MADAME TORTOISE (Rola)
COURT POET (Demoke)
HIS NOVICE
MATA KHARIBU
A CAPTAIN (the Dead Man)
HIS WIFE (the Dead Woman)
PHYSICIAN
HISTORIAN (Adenebi)
SLAVE-DEALER
SOOTHSAYER (Agboreko)
A PAGE, GUARDS, ATTENDANTS, etc.

From ARONI, the Lame One, this testimony . . .

'I know who the Dead Ones are. They are the guests of the Human Community who are neighbours to us of the Forest. It is their Feast, the Gathering of the Tribes. Their councillors met and said, Our forefathers must be present at this Feast. They asked us for ancestors, for illustrious ancestors, and I said to FOREST HEAD, let me answer their request. And I sent two spirits of the restless dead . . .

'THE DEAD MAN, who in his former life was a captain in the army of Mata Kharibu, and the other, . . . THE DEAD WOMAN, in former life, the captain's wife. Their choice was no accident. In previous life they were linked in violence and blood with four of the living generation. The most notorious of them is ROLA, now, as before, a whore. And inevitably she has regained the name by which they knew her centuries before—MADAME TORTOISE. Another link of the two dead with the present is ADENEBI, the Court Orator, oblivious to the real presence of the dead. In previous life he was COURT HISTORIAN. And I must not forget DEMOKE, the Carver. In the other life, he was a POET in the court of Mata Kharibu. AGBOREKO, the Elder of Sealed Lips performed the rites and made sacrifices to Forest Head. His trade was the same in the court of Mata Kharibu. When the guests had broken the surface of earth, I sat and watched what the living would do.

'They drove them out. So I took them under my wing. They became my guests and the Forests consented to dance for them. Forest Head, the one who we call OBANEJI, invited Demoke, Adenebi, and Rola to be present at the dance. They followed him, unwillingly, but they had no choice.

'It was not as dignified a Dance as it should be. ESHUORO had come howling for vengeance and full of machinations. His professed wrongs are part of the story.

'Eshuoro is the wayward flesh of ORO—Oro whose agency serves much of the bestial human, whom they invoke for terror. OGUN, they deify, for his playground is the battle field, but he loves the anvil and protects all carvers, smiths, and all workers in metal.

'For this Feast of the Human Community their Council also resolved that a symbol of the great re-union be carved. Demoke, son of the Old Man, was elected to carve it. Undoubtedly Ogun possessed him for Demoke chose, unwisely, to carve Oro's sacred tree, *araba*. Even this might have passed unnoticed by Oro if Demoke had left araba's height undiminished. But Demoke is a victim of giddiness and cannot gain araba's heights. He would shorten the tree, but apprentice to him is one OREMOLE, a follower of Oro who fought against this sacrilege to his god. And Oremole won support with his mockery of the carver who was tied to earth. The apprentice began to work above his master's head; Demoke reached a hand and plucked him down . . . the final link was complete—the Dance could proceed.'

PART ONE

An empty clearing in the forest. Suddenly the soil appears to be breaking and the head of the Dead Woman pushes its way up. Some distance from her, another head begins to appear, that of a man. They both come up slowly. The man is fat and bloated, wears a dated warrior's outfit, now mouldy. The woman is pregnant. They come up, appear to listen. They do not seem to see each other. Shortly after, Adenebi enters. He passes close to the Dead Man.

DEAD MAN: Will you take my case, sir?

    [*Adenebi starts, stares, and runs off.*]

DEAD MAN: [*shaking his head.*] I thought we were expected.

    [*They both seem to attempt to sense their surrounding.*]

DEAD WOMAN: This is the place.

DEAD MAN: ... Unless of course I came up too soon. It is such a long time and such a long way.

DEAD WOMAN: No one to meet me. I know this is the place.

    [*Obaneji enters, passes close by the woman.*]

DEAD WOMAN: Will you take my case?

    [*Obaneji stops and looks thoughtfully at them. The Dead Man, listening hard, goes quickly towards him. Obaneji withdraws, looking back at the pair.*]

DEAD WOMAN: I thought he might. He considered it long enough.

    [*Demoke enters. He is tearing along.*]

DEAD WOMAN: Will you take my case?

DEMOKE: [*stops.*] Can't you see? I am in a hurry.

DEAD WOMAN: But you stopped. Will you not take my case?

DEMOKE: When you see a man hurrying, he has got a load on his back. Do you think I live emptily that I will take another's cause for pay or mercy?

DEAD WOMAN: And yet we'll meet there.
DEMOKE: You say you know. I am merely on my business. [*Going.*]
DEAD WOMAN: Stop. I lived here once.
DEMOKE: That was before my time. [*Going, stops again.*] Perhaps we will meet. But the reveller doesn't buy a cap before he's invited.

[*Goes. The Dead Woman shakes her head sadly. Rola enters, swinging her hips.*]

DEAD MAN: Madam please, will you take my case?
ROLA: Even before you ask it.
DEAD MAN: [*gladly.*] Will you?
ROLA: [*who has gone nearer him.*] Oh! [*She backs away.*] What is the matter with you!
DEAD MAN: Don't ask.
ROLA: [*stamps her foot angrily.*] What is the matter with you?
DEAD MAN: [*writhing.*] Do I have to answer?
ROLA: You look disgusting. I suppose you are not even a man at all.

[*The dead man turns away. His head falls forward on his chest.*]

ROLA: What a nerve you have. Do you think because you are out of town you, in your condition, can stop me and talk to me? Next time I'll get people to flog you. [*She goes off.*]
DEAD MAN: [*swaying unhappily.*] O O O I am so ashamed. To be found out like that, so soon, so soon. I am so ashamed.
DEAD WOMAN: Could it be I am not qualified after all? After a hundred generations, it is rather difficult to know.
DEAD MAN: I am so ashamed, so ashamed...
DEAD WOMAN: I know they told me to come. I know I was summoned. What is it to them from whom I descended—if that is why they shun me now? The world is big but the dead are bigger. We've been dying since the beginning;

of the Forests 5

the living try but the gap always widens. What is it to them from whom I descended!

DEAD MAN: It was a mistake from the beginning. It is a long way to travel the understreams to be present where the living make merry. What is it to me? I want nothing more. Nothing at all.

DEAD WOMAN: I have been made a fool. It is a hard thing to carry this child for a hundred generations. And I thought... when I was asked, I thought... here was a chance to return the living to the living that I may sleep lighter. [*Sound of bells, shouts, gunshots from afar. The Dead Man listens.*]

DEAD MAN: That is hardly the sound of welcome.

DEAD WOMAN: They would never have tempted me another way. It is a hard thing to lie with the living in your grave.

DEAD MAN: [*still listening.*] Anyway, I have forgotten the procedure. I will only betray myself a stranger. [*Goes.*]

DEAD WOMAN: [*hears the noise.*] Not the procession of welcome. [*Going.*] I've been made a fool. Again. [*Goes off, same direction.*]

[*The noise, very much like that of beaters, comes quite near the clearing. Gunshots are let off, bells rung, etc. It builds to a crescendo and then dies off in the distance. Enter the four who passed by the dead pair—Rola, Adenebi, Obaneji, Demoke.*]

ROLA: ... So I told her to get out. Get out and pack your things. Think of it. Think of it yourself. What did she think I was? I can't take anyone who happens to wander in, just because she claims to be my auntie. My auntie!

ADENEBI: It is rather difficult. I suppose one has to be firm. You start your own family, expect to look after your wife and children, lead—you know—a proper family life. Privacy... very important... some measure of privacy.

But how do you manage that when a lot of brats are delivered at your door because their great grandparents happen to have been neighbours of your great grand-uncles.

ROLA: This whole family business sickens me. Let everybody lead their own lives. [*Throws away her cigarette and takes another.*]

OBANEJI: It never used to be a problem.

ROLA: It is now.

OBANEJI: People like you made it so.

ROLA: Hm. I see we've got another of the good old days.

OBANEJI: On the contrary . . .

ROLA: Never mind. You'd only waste your breath anyway.

[*By now they've seated themselves on tree-trunks, stones, etc.*]

ROLA: The whole sentimentality cloys in my face. That is why I fled. The whole town reeks of it . . . The gathering of the tribes! Do you know how many old and forgotten relations came to celebrate?

OBANEJI: Now we've got it. They pushed you out of house.

ROLA: I've a mind to go back and set fire to it. If I haven't got a house, they can't stay with me.

DEMOKE: It's a good thing in a way. I mean, as long as they don't do it too often. I am sure none of them had ever been down here before.

ROLA: O . . . oh. The silent one has broken his vow. I suppose you wouldn't like to come and live with a pack of dirty, yelling grandmas and fleabitten children?

[*Demoke remains silent.*]

ROLA: I thought not.

DEMOKE: Don't jump to conclusions. I suddenly realized that I was foolish to talk. When the cockerel decides it's fire burning on his head, the only thing to do is pour water on it. [*Obaneji smiles; Rola splutters and crushes her cigarette.*]

OBANEJI: You are the carver, aren't you?

DEMOKE: How did you know?
OBANEJI: [*laughs.*] Look at your hands.
[*Demoke has been shaping a piece of wood with a stone.*]
DEMOKE: As the saying goes, if the red monkey only tumbled in his parlour, no one would know he had any sons.
ADENEBI: Are you *the* carver?
DEMOKE: I am.
ADENEBI: So you are the man. Why aren't you in town? Today is your day of triumph, sir. Every neck is creaking with looking up at the totem.
ROLA: [*wide-eyed.*] Oh. So you did that?
OBANEJI: Unfortunately I have seen so much and I am rarely impressed by anything. But that . . . it was the work of ten generations. I think your hands are very old. You have the fingers of the dead.
ROLA: [*with unexpected solemnity*.] And you did not even cut it down. Climbing the king of trees and carving it as it stood —I think that was very brave.
OBANEJI: It is the kind of action that redeems mankind, don't you think so?
ROLA: But how did you work on it? Did you use ladders and nets or did you straddle it like a palm wine tapper?
DEMOKE: [*with sudden irritation.*] The knife doesn't carve its own handle you know. There were others who lopped off the branches and skinned the trunk. In fact it took quite a few of us to do it. And one man fell to his death.
ROLA: Oh. Did you see it?
DEMOKE: I was beneath him at the time. He fell right past me. I could have touched him if I wished.
ADENEBI: You must have been glad it wasn't you. But I don't see why you are sitting here. You should be in town drinking in the admiration.
DEMOKE: For one thing, I did not know what it was all about.

The council met and decided that they wanted it done. In secret. The tree was in a grove of *Oro*, so it was possible to keep it hidden. Later I learnt it was meant for the gathering of the tribes. When I finished it, the grove was cleared of all the other trees, the bush was razed and a motor road built right up to it. It looked different. It was no longer my work. I fled from it.

OBANEJI: I merely fled from the noise. I suppose we all did.

ADENEBI: Speak for yourself.

OBANEJI: I am sorry. Why are you here?

ADENEBI: You say you fled. I don't believe it. Especially you, a carver. Have you no sense of history?

ROLA: What history? Or doesn't it matter?

ADENEBI: The accumulated heritage—that is what we are celebrating. Mali. Chaka. Songhai. Glory. Empires. But you cannot feel it, can you?

OBANEJI: But what made you leave it and come to this quiet?

ROLA: He got lost in the maze of purple and gold.

ADENEBI: I have a weak heart. Too much emotion upsets me. This is the era of greatness. Unfortunately it is those who cannot bear too much of it to whom the understanding is given . . . Wait. Listen.   [*Distant noise of bells, shouts, etc.*] *They* know what it is all about. I belong with them. And so do you, if you'd only drop your superior airs and admit it. [*Re-enter the Dead Man and Dead Woman.*]

ROLA: [*takes Demoke by the arm.*] Those obscenities again. Let us wander off by ourselves. The others can deal with them.

DEMOKE: [*rises. Goes towards them.*] I must question them.

ROLA: [*pulling him back.*] What can you want with them? Come with me. What on earth is the matter with you?

ADENEBI: [*leaving quickly.*] I came here to get away from the excitement.

OBANEJI: Anyway, one begins to hear the revellers even from

here. Come on carver, we'll go deeper into the forest.
[He takes Demoke by the hand and leads him firmly away, Rola in tow. The two creatures stop. They want to go after, but the noise which they have just heard is increasing. They turn and go out the way they came.]

*

[A tree trunk to one side of the scene. Murete, a tree-demon, is about to come out of it when he hears some noise. Ducks back. Enter Aroni, the one-legged. He looks as if he is going to hop right past the tree when he stops suddenly and gives it a stout wallop. The tree-demon yelps.]

ARONI: So you are not afraid.

[Murete's head emerges warily.]

MURETE: No. When the leaves tremble it is no concern of the roots.

ARONI: You become more and more human every day. I suppose you took that saying from your friend, Agboreko.

MURETE: *He* at least is amusing. And his language is full of colour.

ARONI: Yes, I can see where the colour has run and left ugly patches on you. Be quiet! You are unreliable Murete. You too meant to leave today. Don't lie.

MURETE: I never denied it.

ARONI: Today, when Forest Head needed you all. You meant to desert him.

MURETE: Today there happens to be much more fun among the living.

ARONI: Among the living? Fool, are you dead then?

MURETE: No, but it is dead enough here. Even my home looks dead. You see how the leaves have served someone for a feast?

ARONI: So I noticed. I thought you did it yourself.

MURETE: What for?

ARONI: So I would think you have moved house.

MURETE: Well, frankly, that is why I stayed on. But I didn't do it myself. Eshuoro came here and bit off the top. Said someone else—some woodcutter or something—had cut off his own, so he came to take it out on me.

ARONI: Hm. So that's it. He is sulking somewhere. I was wondering why we hadn't seen him for a while.

MURETE: I'll do him a mischief one of these days.

ARONI: Don't boast uselessly. Murete, I want you at the feast.

MURETE: The welcoming of the dead? No, I am going to drink millet wine at the feast of the living.

ARONI: Doesn't Agboreko bring you enough?

MURETE: Only when he remembers. And then he brings too much and the ants get the rest. I can take my own measure at their feasting.

ARONI: Villain!

MURETE: These rites of the dead, I don't know why you take them on.

ARONI: Do not question. You have not done your share.

MURETE: You wanted witnesses. I guided four human beings towards you.

ARONI: [*lifting up a mighty fist.*] You did what?

MURETE: Well, they passed by me and didn't miss their way. So you might almost say I provided them.

ARONI: Come out. Come out at once.

[*Murete gingerly pops up his head. Comes out, sheepish-impudent.*]

ARONI: [*eyes him sternly.*] I could force you to stay, you know that.

[*Murete maintains a stubborn silence.*]

ARONI: You say you saw four human beings. Did you notice anyone else?

MURETE: Which others?

ARONI: The two dead. The ones they asked for, and no longer want.

of the Forests

MURETE: I did not see them. Do you think I never go to sleep?

ARONI: One more impertinence out of you and I'll tie you backwards and leave you with your tongue licking the earthworm's discharge at every fall of a leaf.

MURETE: It won't be the first time.

ARONI: Take care how you tempt me. I have some more questions. If you answer them sanely, you may save your skin. Now which of the townspeople did you talk to?

MURETE: The one who summoned me, naturally.

ARONI: [*bellows.*] And who was that?

MURETE: [*instinctively raises his arms for protection.*] Agboreko. Their Elder of Sealed Lips.

ARONI: No one else?

MURETE: No one.

ARONI: Not even the Old Man, their Councillor?

MURETE: He never comes himself. Always he sends Agboreko.

ARONI: What did he complain of?

MURETE: How you tricked them. He said they asked Forest Father for illustrious ancestors and you sent them accusers. He wanted to know what lay in your mind.

ARONI: ... And did he?

MURETE: How could he? I don't know myself do I?

ARONI: You are a bad liar. And you also take bribes.

MURETE: I told him to ask you.

ARONI: You said four human beings passed by you. That means you were drunk.

MURETE: Why?

ARONI: Or else you had no eyes in your head. You should have recognized the fourth.

MURETE: Maybe I was sleepy.

ARONI: Be quiet. When last did you see Ogun?

MURETE: Not for a long time.

ARONI: If he comes to you, let me know at once. One of the three witnesses is his servant. I don't want interference from him.

MURETE: What does that mean?

ARONI: Don't leave your house for the moment. I'll send word when you may go on your debauchery.

[*Exit Aroni. Murete makes a rude sign, re-enters the tree. Enter Agboreko, Elder of the Sealed Lips. He wears a white agbada and a white wrapper. Carries a clay pot full of millet wine. A bulky, unhurried man.*]

AGBOREKO: [*sprinkles some of the wine at the foot of the tree and leaves the pot beside it.*] It is I, Agboreko. Murete, it is Agboreko that calls you. Ear that never shuts, eye that never closes. Murete, Agboreko brings you the unhappiness of his children.

MURETE: Come back later. I have told you, the forest is big and I pay no heed to the footsteps of the dead.

AGBOREKO: Murete, if the hunter loses his quarry, he looks up to see where the vultures are circling. Proverb to bones and silence.

MURETE: All right, all right. Come back later. I may have learnt something then.

[*Agboreko sighs, goes. Murete pops up, looks after him.*]

MURETE: [*mimicking.*] Proverb to bones and silence. Somehow I couldn't bear him today. That is Aroni's influence. He spoils everything.

[*Reaches for the pot and takes a deep draught. Enter Ogun who holds the pot against his mouth and forces him to drink the lot at once. Ogun then takes him and turns him quickly round and round. Murete staggers about, quite drunk and unbalanced.*]

OGUN: Drunk again, Murete?

MURETE: [*hiccups. Tries to speak but waffles.*]

OGUN: The four humans—which way did they go?

of the Forests

MURETE: [*points.*]
OGUN: How recently?
MURETE: How... how?
OGUN: Was it a long time?
 [*Murete picks up a leaf. Lets it fall. Takes a twig and breaks it off piece by piece, giggling all the while. Ogun impatiently slaps off his hand.*]
OGUN: You know Demoke, servant of Ogun. Demoke the worker of iron and of wood. Was he among the four?
MURETE: [*drunkenly.*] You.
OGUN: Aroni bade me ask you. He says, was the carver among them? Demoke, the servant of Ogun.
MURETE: You... Ogun... you... Ogun.
OGUN: No you drunkard. Ogun is nowhere here. Aroni sent me. He spoke to you... recently.
MURETE: Yes, yes, Aroni.
OGUN: And Eshuoro, did he speak to you?
MURETE: [*wildly flailing.*] Eshuoro, you bit off my shelter. I'll bite your head off. I'll bite your head off...
OGUN: Gently... gently... of course you'll bite my head off. Don't forget, you are no friend to Eshuoro, are you...?
MURETE: [*baring his teeth.*] I'll bite off yours... come here... just you come here... is it my affair if the woodcutter lopped off your big top. You take up too much room anyway... who do you think you are?
 [*Aims a wild blow at Ogun. He ducks. Murete passes out.*]
OGUN: [*examining him.*] Mm. Mm. [*Props him up against the tree.*] He should bear no love for Eshuoro. It is not much but it is something. Let Eshuoro strip a few more dwellings naked and he won't have a friend at the welcome. Demoke the carver, my friend and servant, it was my axe you drove into araba, pride among the trees of Eshuoro. It was my iron that cicatrized his naked skin—I'll not forget you

Demoke. I shall not forget.

[*Re-enter Obaneji, Demoke, Adenebi and Rola.*]

DEMOKE: They are gone.

OBANEJI: We will follow them if you like.

ROLA: No. Demoke, stay here.

OBANEJI: You really think they are the people your father spoke of?

DEMOKE: I do. Anyway, what does it matter? I still don't know what brought me here.

ADENEBI: Well, don't be over-anxious to find out. At least not from those . . .

DEMOKE: I know we are bound to meet somewhere.

ADENEBI: For heaven's sake let's change the subject.

ROLA: For once I agree with you.

DEMOKE: The man who fell to his death—from the tree—I wonder if he was the other one . . .

ROLA: Dressed like that? For God's sake . . .

ADENIBI: I'm going back if you don't stop this.

OBANEJI: But you said you thought they were the ones Agboreko invoked—at your father's request.

DEMOKE: They say Aroni has taken control. That is when the guilty become afraid.

ROLA: Can't we talk of something else? You . . . you haven't told us why you came. What are you hiding?

OBANEJI: No crime, if that's what you mean. Like your carver here, I was thrown out by the nose. I know too much . . . about people . . . far too much. When I saw them all, actually rejoicing—that much is true at least—most of them did experience joy . . . but you see . . . when they laughed, I was looking down their throats.

ROLA: And what did you see?

OBANEJI: Only what I know already

ROLA: Hm. If it isn't the sage himself.

of the Forests

OBANEJI: Don't misunderstand me. It is just that I work as a filing clerk for the Courts. Senior clerk, mind you. I know about people even before I've met them. Know their whole history sometimes. And against my will, I find that all the time, I am guessing which name belongs to who. You don't know how unnerving that can be, especially when one is so often right.

ROLA: A sort of keeper of the nation's secrets 'eh? What a chance! But I suppose you don't much enjoy it. You only pry against your will.

ADENEBI: [*hurriedly.*] Look, somehow we all seem to be keeping together. So why don't we forget all about unpleasantness?

ROLA: [*coyly at Demoke.*] Do *you* think I was being unpleasant? Anyway, I think people ought to be more honest about their work. I know I would enjoy that sort of thing.

OBANEJI: To be quite honest, I do enjoy some of it. I would never deny that it had its enjoyable side. You know, the lighter side. As I said, we collect records of the most peculiar things. You'd never guess how varied is our collection.

ROLA: I know what *I* would collect mostly.

OBANEJI: Wealthy men?

ROLA: You are turning nasty.

OBANEJI: On the contrary, you suggested we should be more honest towards each other. And I intend to try it out. Now, I for instance. My favourite is motor lorries. You know, passenger lorries. I have a passion for them.

ROLA: What a choice!

OBANEJI: Take one lorry I was examining only yesterday—the records that is—now wait a minute . . . what was the name of it again? I never can remember the number . . . oh yes . . . The Chimney of Ereko.

ADENEBI: That is not its real name.

OBANEJI: Oh, you know it too?

ADENEBI: Of course I do. All the passenger lorries pass through our hands in the council. We perform all the formalities. The name of this one is 'God My Saviour'.

OBANEJI: Yes, that is the name painted on it. But we prefer to call our collection, human or vehicular, by the names by which they are generally known. This one, the Chimney of Ereko. What a lorry! What a record it has. You put it off the road very recently, didn't you?

ADENEBI: We had to. It was smoking like a perpetual volcano.

OBANEJI: Pity. I was very fond of it. Chimney of Ereko. It had survived eight serious crashes, apart from falling in a pit two or three times. Yes, it was something of an old warrior. I grew a real affection for it.

ADENEBI: If you like that sort of thing.

OBANEJI: Oh yes I do. Now take another casebook which we closed only yesterday. Another passenger lorry. They call it the Incinerator.

ADENEBI: Never heard the name.

OBANEJI: You couldn't have. It got that name only yesterday—after what happened.

ROLA: What?

OBANEJI: Before I tell you, I must let you know the history of the lorry. When it was built, someone looked at it, and decided that it would only take forty men. But the owner took it to the council... now, my friend, this is something for you to investigate. One of your office workers took a bribe. A real substantial bribe. And he changed the capacity to seventy.

DEMOKE: Seventy!

OBANEJI: Yes. Seventy. From forty.

ROLA: That's nearly twice.

OBANEJI: You said it—nearly twice. Now what do you think would happen if such a trap suddenly caught fire?

DEMOKE: When?

ROLA: [*shuts her eyes tightly.*] No, no, no, no...

OBANEJI: Yesterday. That is why they have called it the Incinerator since yesterday. Of the seventy people in it, five escaped. It overturned you see, and the body was built of wood.... Dry and brittle in the Harmattan season too. They were all on their way here—to the gathering of the tribes.

[*There is a short silence.*]

ADENEBI: Seventy did you say?

OBANEJI: Excepting five. Only five escaped.

ADENEBI: Seventy. It couldn't have been one of ours.

OBANEJI: Mr. Adenebi. What office do you hold in the council?

ADENEBI: [*angrily.*] What do you imply?

OBANEJI: You misunderstand me. I only meant, are you in a position to find out something for me?

ADENEBI: [*warily.*] That depends. I am only the official Orator to the Council, but...

OBANEJI: You do wield some authority.

ADENEBI: Yes. Certainly.

OBANEJI: You see, I want to close my files on this particular lorry—the Incinerator. And my records won't be complete unless I have the name of the man who did it—you know, the one who took the bribe. Do you think you can help me there?

ADENEBI: Since you are so clever and so knowledgeable, why don't you find that out yourself?

OBANEJI: Please... it is only for the sake of records...

ADENEBI: Then to hell with your records. Have you no feeling for those who died? Are you just an insensitive, inhuman block?

OBANEJI: I didn't kill them. And anyway, we have our different views. The world must go on. After all, what are a mere sixty-five souls burnt to death? Nothing. Your bribe-taker was only a small-time murderer; he wasn't even cold-blooded. He doesn't really interest me very much. I shall be writing his name in small print.

ROLA: He deserves to be hanged.

OBANEJI: Now that's a bloodthirsty woman. No, you cannot really punish the man. After all, how was he to foresee the consequences of his actions? How was he to know that in two months from the deed, the lorry would hit another, overturn completely, and be set on fire?

ROLA: [*fiercely.*] You seem to relish talking about it.

OBANEJI: Oh no. I have seen so much. It simply doesn't impress me, that's all.

[*There is a short silence.*]

DEMOKE: I work with fire. Carving and smelting. Sometimes I merely trace patterns on wood. With fire. I live by the forge and often hold the cinders in my hands. So you see I am not afraid of fire. But I wish to be saved from death by burning. Living, I would rather not watch my body dissolve like alloy. There must be happier deaths.

ROLA: Like what?

OBANEJI: Yes, go on. Tell us. What kind of death would you prefer?

DEMOKE: A fall from a great height.

OBANEJI: [*sharply.*] Why?

DEMOKE: Why?

OBANEJI: Yes, why? Why should you prefer to fall?

DEMOKE: Because I know what it is. I have seen it happen. Didn't I tell you about my apprentice . . .

OBANEJI: Yes, your apprentice. But what has that to do with you?

DEMOKE: I watched it. I took part in it. There is nothing ignoble in a fall from that height. The wind cleaned him as he fell.

And it goes further. I mean, for me, it goes further.
Perhaps it is because I am a slave to heights. You see, I can
go so far so high, but one step further than that and I am
seized with dizziness. Where my hands are burning to
work, where my hands are trembling to mould, my body
will not take me. Is that not a lack of fulfilment? If I can
pull my body up, further than it will go, I would willingly
fall to my death after.

ROLA: That doesn't make sense.

DEMOKE: Oh yes it does. For me it does.

OBANEJI: Hm. And our friend the Orator to the Council...
what sort of death shall we pray that you meet with?

ADENEBI: [*furiously.*] No, you tell us. How would you like to be
killed?

OBANEJI: Oh. I shall have to think a minute or two over that...
Let me see...

ROLA: Why don't you confess it? You are the type who would
rather die in your bed. You look it.

OBANEJI: You say that as if one should be ashamed of it.

ROLA: [*contemptuously.*] No. I suppose there are things which do
crawl into a hole to die.

OBANEJI: [*laughs softly.*] And you? Since the Orator won't tell
us his death-wish, perhaps you will.

ROLA: [*throws her head back and laughs.*] So you'd like to know.
Are you quite sure that you would like to know?

OBANEJI: I asked you, didn't I?

[*Rola swings round suddenly, embraces him and tries to kiss him.*]

OBANEJI: [*struggling.*] Please... please... let me go.

ROLA: Oh no. If you think I am just pretending, go ahead and
kill me right now. You'll see I don't mind at all. Of course,
if I was really going to die, I would go further than that.
[*Obaneji eventually succeeds in throwing her off; Rola loses her
balance and falls. Adenebi runs to assist her to get up.*]

ROLA: Pig! Pig!

ADENEBI: That was quite unnecessary. What sort of a man do you call yourself anyway?

ROLA: [*struggling with Adenebi.*] Let me get at him. I've scratched out duller eyes than yours.

OBANEJI: I am sorry. Believe me, I didn't mean to hurt you.

ROLA: Of course you didn't. You are just naturally uncouth. Pig!

OBANEJI: Again I apologize. But please keep your distance in future. I have a particular aversion to being mauled by women.

ROLA: [*furiously.*] I suppose you weren't born by one. Filth! You should be back among your moths and dust you nosy conceited prig. Who do you think you are anyway, looking perpetually smug and pushing people around?

ADENEBI: I hope you like what you've started. After all you asked the question. You should not complain if you get an unexpected answer.

OBANEJI: You are wrong there. It was not unexpected. It was only the method of reply for which I wasn't prepared.

ROLA: [*looks at him with withering contempt.*] No wonder you were not prepared. I don't suppose you have ever in your life dared to hold a woman in your arms...

OBANEJI: Please... please... let us change the subject.

ROLA: You started it. And anyway who are you to think that we will only talk of whatever happens to please you? I am getting sick of the way you step back when it seems you are about to get splashed, especially as you swing your feet about as much as you do...

OBANEJI: Once again, I am sorry. But please don't...

ROLA: [*teasing, quite bitchily, makes a sudden dart and pulls at his beard.*]
  He'll die in his bed but he'll die alone
  He'll sleep in his bed but he'll sleep alone

of the Forests

He'll wake in the morning and he'll eat alone
So good up in heaven he sang praises alone.

OBANEJI: I beg you not to impress yourself on me so hard. I have told you, recognition is the curse I carry with me. I don't want to know any more. I thought I was safe with you. I thought that you all wanted to be quiet.

DEMOKE: Let me tell you a story. Once upon a time...

ROLA: Shut up. It is he who ought to tell us a story. Let him tell us of his life. How came it he was born not fully formed?

ADENEBI: Really, this is too much. A lady shouldn't...

OBANEJI: I know you already. But do you have to betray yourself to these people?

ROLA: Don't you dare suggest you know me. Whatever it is you keep in your filthy records, I am not in them. I am not a criminal. I don't work in the council and I never drove your Incinerator. I have never been to court in all my life.

OBANEJI: Let me beg you to be quiet then.

ROLA: There is the graveyard. Find yourself a graveyard if you want some silence.

OBANEJI: I don't think that would be any better than here. Isn't the graveyard filled with your lovers?

ROLA: What!

[*There is silence.*]

ADENEBI: Now, really...

OBANEJI: Well, look at her. Doesn't she look the type who would drive men to madness and self-destruction!

ROLA: What do you mean? Say it outright. What do you mean?

OBANEJI: Nothing. I merely hoped that would keep you silent.

ROLA: You have a filthy mind. Coward! Why don't you say what is in your mind?

OBANEJI: I beg you to let us change this subject.

ROLA: Out with it! I have nothing to be ashamed of. Because your ears are stuck to gossip, you throw out perpetual feelers for muck. Do you think I do not know what you meant?

DEMOKE: Why? Why? Why? The man said nothing. Only a feeble effort to be cruel. Why do you take it to heart?

ROLA: Shut up or I'll get those who will tear the skin off your back. You and your complacent friend.

DEMOKE: [*suddenly.*] Madame Tortoise! Blind. Blind. [*Hitting himself on the forehead.*] Madame Tortoise, that is who you are!

[*Rola stands stock-still, her face drained of expression.*]

OBANEJI: [*quietly.*] You've been begging for a stone to hit you on the head. Couldn't you be quiet?

ROLA: [*breaking down.*] What have I done to you? What have I ever done to you?

[*She falls on her knees, still sobbing.*]

ADENEBI: Do you know what you have just said? You had better be sure it is true.

OBANEJI: He seems to know her. I thought she was tougher.

DEMOKE: Madame Tortoise. Just think . . . I have been with her all day . . .

ROLA: [*raises her head suddenly.*] Isn't that enough? Have you all suddenly earned the right to stare at me as if I was leprous? You want me to wallow in self-disgust. Well, I won't. I wasn't made the way you think women are.

ADENEBI: What! No shame. No shame at all.

DEMOKE: Please, don't upset yourself—not over *him*.

ROLA: Ho. You are very kind, are you not? You think you have enough for yourself that you can spare me some pity. Well keep it. Keep it. Just what is it you all accuse me of?

OBANEJI: [*placatingly.*] Nothing. Nothing.

ADENEBI: Nothing? Do you call that nothing? Two lovers in the graveyard. And the sordidness of it. The whole horrible scandal. How did I ever get in your company?

ROLA: Go. It is people like you ... Psh! Since when did I ever begin to waste a glance on fools. You know that, I hope. You are a fool. A foolish man. The word has meaning when I look at you. I wouldn't be sorry to see you under the ground, except that it wouldn't be because you were my lover.

ADENEBI: Her brazenness. Do you see? She is utterly unrepentant!

ROLA: People like you beg to be shaven clean on the skull. Except that I couldn't bear to touch you.

DEMOKE: I carved something to you. Of course I didn't know you then, I mean, I had never met you. But from what I heard, you were so ...

ADENEBI: Bestial. Yes, just the sort of thing you would carve, isn't it? Like your totem. Bestial it was. Utterly bestial.

DEMOKE: Actually, that is what I mean. Madame Tortoise is the totem—most of it anyway. In fact, you might almost say she dominated my thoughts—she, and something else. About equally.

ADENEBI: Something equally revolting I am sure.

DEMOKE: [*simply*.] On no. Equally ... Anyway, it had to do with me.

[*Adenebi sniggers.*]

OBANEJI: One moment. I thought I heard you say, earlier on, that this work was quite remarkable.

ADENEBI: That didn't mean I thought it even worth the trouble. And anyway, we had only met. I wanted to see if he was at all fooled by his own monstrosity.

ROLA: You see. Men like that, who can pity them? Do they not beg that their lives be wrung out of them? That their heads be turned inside out?

ADENEBI: Are you making excuses?

ROLA: Not to you. Not to anyone. I owe all that happened to my nature. I regret nothing. They were fools, fools to think they were something better than . . . the other men. My other men.

ADENEBI: Men! Some of them were hardly grown up. We heard you liked them young, really young.

ROLA: I regret nothing. You men are conceited fools. Nothing was ever done on my account. Nothing. What you do is boost yourselves all the time. By every action. When that one killed the other, was it on my account? When he killed himself, could he claim that he did it for me? He was only big with himself, so leave me out of it.

ADENEBI: I suppose you didn't really run merely because you were beset by your relations. They simply didn't leave you room to entertain your lovers. And this could have been a profitable season. A generous season.

ROLA: Draw your filthy conclusions. I only know I am master of my fate. I have turned my training to good account. I am wealthy, and I know where my wealth came from.

ADENEBI: Oh yes, you ruined countless. Young and old. Old, peaceful ones who had never even set eyes on you; who simply did not know what their son was up to; didn't know he was draining the home away—for you.

ROLA: Don't go on or you'll make me cry. Fool! What is it to me? When your business men ruin the lesser ones, do you go crying to them? I also have no pity for the one who invested foolishly. Investors, that is all they ever were—to me.

OBANEJI: [*nodding, with a faint faraway smile.*] Madame Tortoise . . . Madame Tortoise . . . Do you realize, I even knew your ancestors. I knew . . .

ROLA: And you, I suppose you have no ancestors. You are merely the dust that came off a moth's wing.

[*Obaneji appears to be shut up by this. There is an uncomfortable silence.*]

of the Forests

DEMOKE: You don't look one bit similar to your other face—you know, the one that rises from legends. That was the one I thought of. I thought of you together, but... you are not the same. Anyway, you can have a look at my totem and tell me. I needed some continuity and you provided it— You do see why, don't you? I take it you do know of the legendary Madame Tortoise.

ROLA: [*subdued.*] No. What was she?

DEMOKE: [*shrugs.*] A woman.

ADENEBI: [*rises.*] I think I must leave your company. He talks like a lost lunatic and you are worse than the devil. I don't want to be involved in your types.

[*Goes off. Rushes back immediately and goes off the opposite way. The Dead Pair enter.*]

OBANEJI: Perhaps we ought to go too.

[*Demoke rises sharply. Goes to the Dead Man.*]

DEMOKE: Are you the one who fell from the tree?

ROLA: Use your eyes. He cannot be. Come away for heaven's sake.

DEMOKE: Did you meet? Does he accuse me?

DEAD MAN: I always did want to come here. This is my home. I have always yearned to come back. Over there, nothing held me. I owned nothing, had no desire to. But the dark trees and the thick earth drew me. When I died, I fell into the understreams, and the great summons found me ready. I travelled the understreams beneath the great ocean; I travelled the understreams beneath the great seas. I flowed through the hardened crust of this oldest of the original vomits of Forest Father...

DEMOKE: And did you meet Oremole the bonded carver? Does he accuse me?

OBANEJI: Must you be in such haste? Everything will come to you sooner or later.

DEAD MAN: [*jerks up suddenly.*] Like palsy. How suddenly you shake with violence!

DEAD WOMAN: What is this? The one who was to take my case—has he sent another down? Into the pit?

DEAD MAN: What have they thought that it fills the air so suddenly with stench?

DEAD WOMAN: A hundred generations has made no difference. I was a fool to come.

DEAD MAN: It is death you reek of. Now I know what the smell is.

DEMOKE: I did ... I asked you, did he accuse me?

DEAD WOMAN: I said the living would save me. What fingers are these whom I begged to let down my child, gently? What have you thought to push me further down the pit? [*Goes.*]

DEAD MAN: May you be cursed again. May you be cursed again. [*Goes.*]

DEMOKE: I pushed him. I pushed him down.

ROLA: Who?

DEMOKE: He climbed higher and I pushed him down. The one who did not fall from the tree. Apprentice to my craft, till I plunged him into hell.

OBANEJI: Save it. Save it for later.

ROLA: Leave him alone. What is it all to you?

OBANEJI: He needn't speak. Why does he? Why do you all? I want nothing, asked nothing.

DEMOKE: Now, now, and from his nest, I will again
Pluck him, Oremole servant of Oro, and fling him,
Screaming downwards into hell.

OBANEJI: Hatred. Pride. Blindness. Envy. Was it envy?

DEMOKE: Envy, but not from prowess of his adze.
The world knew of Demoke, son and son to carvers;
Master of wood, shaper of iron, servant of Ogun,
Slave, alas, to height, and the tapered end
Of the silk-cotton tree. Oremole

My bonded man, whetted the blades,
Lit the fires to forge Demoke's tools.
Strong he was; he whirled the crooked wheel
When Oro puffed himself, Oro who was born
With a pebble in his throat, and frightens children
Begging for their tiny hands to pull it out.
Oremole was the cat by night. The cloth that hangs
Above tall branches, Oremole left it there.
Nimble like a snake, he had no foot to trip him.
And now he sat above my head, carving at the head
While I crouched below him, nibbling hairs
Off the chest of *araba*, king among the trees.
So far could I climb, one reach higher
And the world was beaten like an egg and I
Clasped the tree-hulk like a lover.
Thrice I said I'll cut it down, thread it,
Stride it prostrate, mould and master *araba*
Below the knee, shave and scrape him clean
On the head. But thrice Oremole, slave,
Server to Eshuoro laughed! 'Let me anoint
The head, and do you, my master, trim the bulge
Of his great bottom.' The squirrel who dances on
A broken branch, must watch whose jaws are open
Down below. Thrice I said I would behead it
Where my feet would go no further. Thrice
Oremole, slave, fawner on Eshuoro laughed.
'No one reduces Oro's height, while I serve
The wind. Watch Oremole ride on Aja's head,
And when I sift the dust, master, gather it
Below.' The water-pot, swept up suddenly
Boasted, Aja is my horse. Has it got wings
Or is it not made of clay? I plucked him down!
Demoke's head is no woman's cloth, spread

To receive wood shavings from a carpenter.
Down, down I plucked him, screaming on Oro.
Before he made hard obeisance to his earth,
My axe was executioner at Oro's neck. Alone,
Alone I cut the strands that mocked me, till head
And boastful slave lay side by side, and I
Demoke, sat on the shoulders of the tree,
My spirit set free and singing, my hands,
My father's hands possessed by demons of blood
And I carved three days and nights till tools
Were blunted, and these hands, my father's hands
Swelled big as the tree-trunk. Down I came
But Ogun touched me at the forge, and I slept
Weary at his feet.

MAN'S VOICE: [*quite near.*] Demoke!
OBANEJI: Who was that?
VOICE: Demoke!
OBANEJI: Do you know that voice?
DEMOKE: My father's.
OBANEJI: Quickly then. This way. It came from here.
[*He leads them in the wrong direction.
Enter Ogun. Rapidly.*]
OGUN: Once again, he foiled me. Forest Father,
Deeper still you lead my ward into your
Domain, where I cannot follow. To stay him,
I assumed his father's voice, who follows now
Hard upon my heels. I'll not desert him.
The crime, if crime it was, lies on my head.
My instrument he was, plucking out Oremole
Worshipper of Oro, slayer of my disciples.
I set his hand to the act. I killed
The proud one, who would not bow araba's head
When the gifted hands of Demoke, son and son

> To carvers would pass his spirit into wood.
> Would master wood with iron, fibre with fire!
> Forest Father, masquerading as a human,
> Bringing them to judgement, I'll not desert
> My servant. I am no less son to you than others
> And if my voice is not heard, my hand must
> Be felt.
>
> [*The beaters' noise comes over, increasing during Ogun's speech. He goes off as the Old Man, followed by two of the councillors, enters, surrounded by the whole chaos of beaters.*]

OLD MAN: You are sure it wasn't my son Demoke?

COUNCILLOR: Very sure. I am absolutely certain.

OLD MAN: Anyway, you say the person was heading for home.

COUNCILLOR: It was Adenebi, the Court Orator. I couldn't mistake him.

OLD MAN: Never mind. I'm only worried because he went into hiding. But I don't think he would wander into the forest. I begged him not to.

[*Adenebi enters.*]

COUNCILLOR: That's the man himself. I thought I saw you returning home.

ADENEBI: So I was. And then I heard all the commotion. And I met one of your men who said you were hunting some shady characters.

OLD MAN: And so we are.

ADENEBI: What are they like?

OLD MAN: I don't know. I haven't seen them.

ADENEBI: But in that case...

OLD MAN: Look here, we haven't got nets or cages, so you can see we are not really trying to capture them. If we can drive them away from here, it will be sufficient. [*To the Councillor.*] Tell the men to scatter. They are not covering sufficient ground. They must move wider. I can't hear them. I cannot hear them. They must make a lot more noise.

ADENEBI: Won't they get away before you...

OLD MAN: My friend, we want them to go; to go before we get there, wherever there is. And if the guest won't go quietly, we must shout out the price of food.

ADENEBI: What guest?

OLD MAN: What guest? Oh, go, go!

ADENEBI: I'm sorry, but if you will talk in riddles... Talking about guests, what about the half dozen or so special guests whom we were supposed to expect.

OLD MAN: [*very restlessly.*] They are the very people we are trying to drive off.

ADENEBI: What! What kind of welcome is that?

OLD MAN: Look. Go on, look. Do I seem mad?

ADENEBI: No.

OLD MAN: Well, believe me when I tell you that everything has misfired. These people who have come to claim our hospitality do not wish us well. We were sent the wrong people. We asked for statesmen and we were sent executioners.

[*One of the crowd enters.*]

ADENEBI: I don't understand. I thought we left it all to you.

OLD MAN: Ah, petrol. You, get me one of the councillors.

[*The man goes.*] I have just remembered. They cannot stand the smell of petrol.

[*Councillor enters.*]

Get some petrol. Pour it all over the forest. They cannot stand the smell.

COUNCILLOR: Baba, don't you think that...

OLD MAN: Now what am I thinking of? I must be getting tired. No sensible man burns the house to cook a little yam. I

of the Forests

know what I want. Remember the old decrepit wagon we put off the road?

COUNCILLOR: Oh. The Chimney of Ereko?

OLD MAN: That's the one. Tell the owner it is back on the road—in the forest, that is. Get him to drive it right through here and he can let it smoke as much as he likes. Fill up his tank and charge it to the council.

COUNCILLOR: Baba, no vehicle could move a foot in this bush.

OLD MAN: The Chimney can. He's survived at least half a dozen head-on crashes; not to mention the number of houses he's knocked down for being too near the street. Don't worry, it will tame this jungle.

[*The councillor goes.*]

ADENEBI: Sir, will you kindly explain what is happening?

OLD MAN: [*not listening.*] Yes, yes, the Chimney ought to do it. When that monster travels at anything over two miles per hour you can't see the world for smoke or smell a latrine for petrol fumes. If any ghost can survive it, then there is no power that can help me.

ADENEBI: Sir, I am still waiting for some sort of explanation. I know I am not dreaming.

OLD MAN: What is the matter with you? [*Looks up as if he is seeing him for the first time.*]

ADENEBI: Nothing I hope. But such a lot seems to be happening. Just tell me one thing. Did I or did I not hear aright when you said that all this was to drive off the very people we had invited to be our guests?

OLD MAN: Yes.

ADENEBI: I beg your pardon sir. Did you say 'Yes'?

OLD MAN: Yes, yes, yes!

ADENEBI: But . . . but . . . this is madness.

OLD MAN: Why? Was it or was it not you who spoke in favour of my idea in the council? Did you not threaten to finance the whole programme yourself if the council turned it down?

ADENEBI: Certainly I did. It fell to me as official Orator.

OLD MAN: Well then, are you backing out now?

ADENEBI: [*completely flabbergasted.*] But . . . I don't see how . . . wait a minute. Let me understand where I am. I remember what I said, what we promised to do. An occasion such as the gathering of the tribes—a great thing . . . it would happen only once in several lifetimes . . . only once in centuries of history. It is a whole historical epoch in itself. We resolved to carve a totem, a totem that would reach to the sky.

OLD MAN: Yes. My son carved it.

ADENEBI: Your son? Was that your son?

OLD MAN: Yes, don't look so surprised. We come from a long line of carvers.

ADENEBI: Oh. Well, in addition I said; . . . no, you said, and I took it up, that we must bring home the descendants of our great forebears. Find them. Find the scattered sons of our proud ancestors. The builders of empires. The descendants of our great nobility. Find them. Bring them here. If they are half-way across the world, trace them. If they are in hell, ransom them. Let them symbolize all that is noble in our nation. Let them be our historical link for the season of rejoicing. Warriors. Sages. Conquerors. Builders. Philosophers. Mystics. Let us assemble them round the totem of the nation and we will drink from their resurrected glory.

OLD MAN: Yes. It was a fine speech. But control, at some point was lost to our enemies. The guests we were sent are slaves and lackeys. They have only come to undermine our strength. To preach to us how ignoble we are. They are disgruntled creatures who have come to accuse their

of the Forests

superiors as if this were a court of law. We have courts for the oppressed. Let them go somewhere else.

ADENEBI: I see. I had thought how splendid it would all be. Purple robes. White horses dressed in gold. Processions through the town with communion and service around our symbol . . . by the way, I really ought to tell you how disappointed I was with your son's handiwork. Don't you think it was rather pagan? I should have thought that something more in keeping with our progress would be more appropriate.

OLD MAN: You should have told him.

ADENEBI: I never saw it till it was finished. In fact I saw the carver himself—your son—only today. But I didn't have time to tell him . . .

OLD MAN: Did you say you saw him? When?

ADENEBI: Not very long ago. There were two other people at the time. Strange people.

OLD MAN: [*thoughtfully.*] I fear for him. I greatly fear for him.

ADENEBI: Why? Is he unwell? He seemed quite healthy when we . . .

OLD MAN: No, no. It is nothing. Forget I spoke.

[*Enter the Councillor.*]

OLD MAN: Will he do it?

COUNCILLOR: Yes. He's on his way.

OLD MAN: I hope he kills them all over again. [*Angrily.*] Slaves! Can't they forget they once had lives of their own? How dare they pester the living with the petty miseries of their lives!

ADENEBI: Mali. Songhai. Perhaps a descendant of the great Lisabi. Zimbabwe. Maybe the legendary Prester John himself. . . . I was thinking of heroes like they.

OLD MAN: Isn't it time Agboreko was back? If he has learnt nothing by now then the whole Forest is against us.

COUNCILLOR: He went to consult Murete of the Trees.

OLD MAN: Hm. It shows how helpless we are. Murete, the most unreliable of the tree demons, but he is the only one who will even respond when he is called. It serves me right. The cricket didn't know he was well off until he asked the sparrow to admire his hole.

ADENEBI: Mali. Songhai. Lisabi. Prester John . . . but who did we get?

OLD MAN: Nonentities without a doubt. It is only the cockroach who shouts vanity when the chicken struts.

AGBOREKO: [*entering.*] Proverb to bones and silence.

OLD MAN: Agboreko. At last.

AGBOREKO: I heard them again.

OLD MAN: Was there some change?

AGBOREKO: They notice nothing. They are so full of themselves and their grievances. The worst possible type to deal with.

OLD MAN: They won't go among the people will they?

AGBOREKO: It won't be necessary. Aroni has taken them under his wing. And anyway, they have met one of their old adversaries. Madame Tortoise.

COUNCILLOR: The one who still bears that name?

AGBOREKO: The same. And that is one descendant we overlooked. Illustrious too beyond a doubt. And they are strongly linked to her. Through what crime, I do not know.

OLD MAN: And where does Aroni mean to hold court? If we knew that . . .

AGBOREKO: If the flea had a home of his own, he wouldn't be out on a dog's back. Proverb to bones and silence.

OLD MAN: And Murete . . . wouldn't tell?

AGBOREKO: Nine times I asked Murete of the trees. And nine times he said to me, Aroni will tell you. Ask him.

OLD MAN: Well, ask him.

AGBOREKO: [*shakes his head.*] Aroni is Wisdom itself. When he

of the Forests

means to expose the weaknesses of human lives, there is nothing can stop him. And he knows how to choose his time.

OLD MAN: [*drawing him aside.*] Oremole... the one who... fell from the tree. Is he among the dead?

AGBOREKO: Not yet. Perhaps not at all.

OLD MAN: And would the others accuse on his behalf?

AGBOREKO: The lips of the dead did not open thus far. I cannot tell.

OLD MAN: Does the Old Man of the Forest himself pass judgement or is it his wayward court?

AGBOREKO: Would that affect the scales of Aroni? The chameleon dances, his father claps and you exclaim, 'How modestly the young one keeps silence.' Proverb to bones and silence.

COUNCILLOR: There is still hope. We have heard nothing of Forest Father. Perhaps Aroni merely acts on his own.

AGBOREKO: [*shakes his head.*] Oro cried last night and Bashiru vanished from his bed. Do you still wonder what became of your friend? Proverb to bones and silence.

COUNCILLOR: I am sorry.

ADENEBI: But where does your Forest Father come in? Who is he anyway?

[*There is total silence while they all stare at him.*]

AGBOREKO: [*sighs.*] Perhaps I should go and summon Murete once more. He might have eaten by now.

OLD MAN: [*quickly.*] Agboreko, pay no attention to...

AGBOREKO: Did you think I took notice? Because it rained the day the egg was hatched the foolish chicken swore he was a fish. Proverb to bones and silence. [*Goes.*]

OLD MAN: [*shouts after him.*] Offer Murete millet wine for a whole year.

ADENEBI: I don't think my place is here. Perhaps this is some sort of play for the gathering, but I am too busy to worry my head a moment longer about all this mystery. I can see now that the carver is your son . . . such peculiar behaviour.

OLD MAN: You should go. And if you see my son again tell him not to forget what I told him.

ADENEBI: You'll probably run into him yourself. He is still somewhere around here.

OLD MAN: Here? In the bush? [*Adenebi is going.*] Wait! Did you say you saw my son here?

ADENEBI: I told you. I was with him.

OLD MAN: But here? In the forest? [*Angrily.*] Why didn't you tell me that before?

ADENEBI: You didn't ask.

OLD MAN: Forgive me. Were there others?

ADENEBI: Yes. One man, and another, a woman. I was fourth.

OLD MAN: Was it near here?

ADENEBI: [*looks around.*] Yes. In fact I think we rested in this clearing for some time.

OLD MAN: Did you hear or notice anything?

ADENEBI: Like what?

OLD MAN: Anything! Did you meet other people for instance?

ADENEBI: There was nobody else . . . oh no . . . there were two mad creatures . . . you know, those mad people you find everywhere. They were very unpleasant looking. In fact, it was the reason why I decided to go back. They seemed to follow us all over the place. They made me feel like vomiting. Oh yes, and I found that the woman who was with us was that notorious lady they call Madame Tortoise. That was really why I left. Think, if I, a councillor, was discovered with her!

OLD MAN: [*agitatedly.*] Madame Tortoise! And my son was with you?

ADENEBI: He was.

OLD MAN: Who was the fourth?

ADENEBI: I don't know. An impertinent old man. Said he was a Chief Clerk or something.

OLD MAN: I feared it. Eshuoro was the fourth. Eshuoro must have been the fourth, leading you all to your destruction. How did you escape him?

ADENEBI: I . . . I don't know . . . What is this?

OLD MAN: A servant of Oro was killed. Nothing will rest until we are all bathed in blood. . . . [*Raises his voice suddenly.*] Agboreko! Agboreko—o!

[*Agboreko hurries in almost at once.*]

AGBOREKO: They passed here. They stayed at this very spot and spoke with four people.

OLD MAN: I shouted to tell you the same. Something Adenebi said awoke all the suspicions in me. And my son was among the four. With Madame Tortoise. Did you not know that?

AGBOREKO: Murete consented at last to unseal his lips. Two of the dead spoke to four people; they wanted human advocates.

OLD MAN: At whose prompting?

AGBOREKO: No doubt it is another cunning thought of Aroni. To let the living condemn themselves.

OLD MAN: [*pointing to Adenebi.*] He was with them. Why? What has he ever done?

ADENEBI: Don't class me with Madame Tortoise. I am no murderer . . .

AGBOREKO: He is still in the forest isn't he? It will all come out.

ADENEBI: [*frightened.*] Don't speak of me at all. Leave me out of your thoughts altogether.

AGBOREKO: Anyway, the man is a fool. Is that not enough **crime for Aroni?**

OLD MAN: The fourth. Who was the fourth then? There were four of them.

AGBOREKO: Until the last gourd has been broken, let us not talk of drought. Proverbs to bones and silence. [*Beaters' noises audible again.*]

OLD MAN: Then you too have thought the same. Eshuoro it must have been.

AGBOREKO: A hundred and twenty-one of the sons and servants of Forest Father it could have been. Even the Father of Forests himself. Let us be busy. I have sent for my man.

OLD MAN: Yes, yes. They passed here. He says they passed here and stayed a while. If we drive off the witnesses Aroni has no power. Where is your man? Isn't he here yet?

AGBOREKO: He is on his way.

[*Definite rhythm of drums above beaters' noises.*]

OLD MAN: He'll come too late.

AGBOREKO: No. Patience, Baba. Patience.

ADENEBI: Who is this man? Shall we send somebody for him? I will go if you like.

AGBOREKO: If the wind can get lost in the rainstorm it is useless to send him an umbrella. Proverb to bones and silence.

OLD MAN: Yes, yes, we'll be patient.

AGBOREKO: The eye that looks downwards will certainly see the nose. The hand that dips to the bottom of the pot will eat the biggest snail. The sky grows no grass but if the earth called her barren, it will drink no more milk. The foot of the snake is not split in two like a man's or in hundreds like the centipede's, but if Agere could dance patiently like the snake, he will uncoil the chain that leads into the dead . . .

[*Enter the beaters, shouting. The flogger immediately breaks through them and sets out to clear a space with his long whip, which he freely exercises. The dancer follows almost at once, followed by his acolyte (a very intense young girl). She sprinkles*

of the Forests

the cleared space after the flogger. The dirge-man begins to recite within a few minutes of their entry. An assistant hands Agboreko the divination board, the bowl and kernels.]

DIRGE-MAN: Move on eyah! Move apart
I felt the wind breathe—no more
Keep away now. Leave the dead
Some room to dance.

If you see the banana leaf
Freshly fibrous like a woman's breasts
If you see the banana leaf
Shred itself, thread on thread
Hang wet as the crêpe of grief
Don't say it's the wind. Leave the dead
Some room to dance.

[Agboreko has already cast the kernels. The Old Man goes up inquiringly to him. Agboreko draws lines and pronounces.]
AGBOREKO: The loft is not out of reach when the dust means to settle. Oracle to the living and silence.
[The Old Man turns away, disappointed. The dancer does not, of course, ever stop, although the drumming is lowered for Agboreko, and for the dirge-man.]
DIRGE-MAN: *[goes to the drummer and gives him the two-fisted greeting. The acolyte, who has finished her sprinkling, begins to dance softly, growing rapidly more intense.]*

Ah, your hands are vanished and if it thunders

We know where the hands are gone
But we name no names, let no god think
We spy his envy. Leave the dead
Some room to dance.

[*The process is repeated between Agboreko and the Old Man.*]
AGBOREKO: Have you seen a woman throw away her pestle
when she really means to pound yam? When Iredade took
her case to Orunmila, he said, If the worm doesn't jig near
the roost, the fowl may still want to peck, but at least it
can't say the worm was throwing dust in his face. Go home
therefore, go home. Iredade turned sadly away so
Orunmila called her back. He said, They say the forest is
more cunning any time of the year, but who ever lay back
in his house and watched the creepers grow over him?
Oracle to the Living and silence.
[*The dirge-man has been circling the acolyte.*]

DIRGE-MAN: Daughter, your feet were shod
In eeled shuttles of Yemoja's loom
But twice your smock went up
And I swear your feet were pounding
Dust at the time. Girl, I know
The games of my ancestors. Leave the dead
Some room to dance.

A touch, at that rounded moment of the night
And the dead return to life
Dum-belly woman, plantain-breasted
Mother! What human husband folds

of the Forests

> His arms, and blesses randy ghosts?
> Keep away now, leave, leave the dead
> Some room to dance.

[*The dirge-man joins one or two others in a casual dance in the background. Agboreko again consults his board and kernels.*]

AGBOREKO: When they heard the thunder, Osumare said, That was only me laughing at mice. If they are the dead and we are the living, then we are their children. They shan't curse us. When the busy-body neighbour said to the child, you haven't been home-trained, the mother went and tore her wrapper. She said it is not my child you cursed, it is I.

OLD MAN: [*very disgruntled.*] Ho, They say when the rock hit the tortoise, he shrugged his shoulder and said, I've always been cracked. When his wife met him, she asked, When did you begin to clatter?

AGBOREKO: [*putting away his bowl.*] Proverb to bones and ... That was thunder!

[*He hastily retrieves his paraphernalia.*]

OLD MAN: No sign of rain. I can't see a cloud, can you?

AGBOREKO: It was thunder. Thunder. I must cast afresh!

[*The rumble which they all heard continues to increase. It soon reveals itself as the roar of a high-powered lorry, bearing down on them, headlights full on.*]

ADENEBI: Look! It is not thunder at all. There is a drunkard at the wheel.

OLD MAN: I sent for it. For fumigation. It is the Chimney of Ereko.

AGBOREKO: The Chimney of Ereko! A-a-ah, Baba, Will you never believe that you cannot get rid of ancestors with the little toys of children ...

A BEATER: The Chimney of Ereko! The Chimney of Ereko!
[*The cry is taken up. Within seconds they have all panicked. They scatter in every direction. Adenebi is knocked down. As he attempts to rise he is knocked down again and trampled by flying feet. Agboreko and the Old Man stand their ground for a while, but Agboreko eventually yields, shouting what is probably a fitting proverb to the Old Man before making a not very dignified exit, but nothing is heard for the roar of the lorry and the panic of the crowd.*
Before Agboreko is out of sight, the Old Man takes another look at the head-lamps and disappears. Adenebi rises slowly. The noise of the engine is quite deafening. He looks round, half-dazed but becomes suddenly active on discovering that he is alone. Runs around shouting names, then turns to run into the headlamps, stops suddenly and stands with raised arms, screaming. There is a crash, the noise stops suddenly, and the lights go out. Adenebi's scream being heard above it and after, stopping suddenly as he hears his own terror in the silence.]
ADENEBI: [*sags slowly to his knees and gropes around.*] ... Demoke, Demoke. Where is that carver! And where is that woman who drains the life from men, slowly or in violence. Madame Tortoise. Madame Tortoise! My friends. My friends ...
[*A slow rumble of scattered voices, and the forest creatures pass through, from the direction of the lorry, coming straight down and turning right and left. They all hold leaves to their noses, and grumble all the way. Some sniff in disgust, others spit, all stop their noses, disapproving strongly of the petrol fumes. Adenebi tries to make himself as inconspicuous as possible. Some fan their faces, and one has encased his head completely in a clay pot. They are all assortments of forest spirits, from olobiribiti, who rolls himself like a ball, to the tow-headed purubororo, whose four horns belch continuous smoke.*]

ADENEBI: [*emerging when all is again quiet. Looks around him.*] I have always lived in mortal terror of being lost.
[*Obaneji, Rola and Demoke enter. They walk across and out on the other side without seeing Adenebi. Obaneji returns at once.*]

OBANEJI: Did you find out?

ADENEBI: [*quickly on the defensive.*] What? What ought I to have found out?

OBANEJI: You promised me. You said you would use your influence. For my records. Who did it? Who burnt out sixty-five souls?

ADENEBI: I . . . do not wish . . . to know you. I want to be left alone.
[*Obaneji turns to go with a shrug.*]

ADENEBI: Wait. I want to find my way out. I am lost here.

OBANEJI: [*pointing to the direction they were taking.*] Not this way. This leads deeper into the forest.

ADENEBI: Where are you taking them?

OBANEJI: To the welcoming of the dead. Your people refuse to acknowledge them. And yet they sacrificed until my dwelling reeked of nothing but sheep's blood and I granted their request. Now they drive them out like thieves. [*Goes.*]
[*Adenebi faces the opposite direction. Takes a step forward, peers into the darkness. Turns and runs after Obaneji.*]

PART TWO

Scene as Murete's dwelling. Murete is about to leave home for the human festivities. Stops to clean his nails against the bark of the tree.

MURETE: [*grumbling.*] Fine time to tell me he no longer needs me. What will I find at this hour but the dregs of emptied pots? If it wasn't considered obscene I would compensate my loss from the palm tree. Can't understand why not. Human beings drink their mother's milk. Drink the milk of mothers other than their own. Drink goat's milk. Cow's milk. Pig's blood. So just because I am Murete of the trees is no reason why I shouldn't climb the palm tree and help myself. I'll do it too. One of these days when I am drunk enough. [*Stops.*] Hm, there doesn't seem to be any sense in that. If I'm drunk, then I am not thirsty, so what would I be doing up the palm? [*Examines his nails with satisfaction. Straightens up his finery.*] But I'll do it just the same. If Aroni likes, he can ostracize me.

[*Eshuoro enters from behind, grasps him by the throat.*]

ESHUORO: Swear, not a word.
MURETE: [*choking.*] I swear.
ESHUORO: Not a word to anyone that you saw me.
MURETE: I swear.
ESHUORO: Swear again. And don't forget that Eshuoro does not forgive the sacrilegious. [*Forces a leaf between his teeth and tears it off.*] Swear!
MURETE: I swear.

[*Eshuoro lets him go, Murete stumbles angrily spitting out the piece of leaf in his mouth.*]

MURETE: [*with impotent fury.*] Have you had your fill of eating

A Dance of the Forests

others' roofs that you now think you can spare Murete a leaf or two of my own house!

ESHUORO: [*looks at the tree.*] That was nothing. And don't make me prove to you it was nothing. Answer quickly. Today is the day, isn't it?

MURETE: So you say. But what day is it, forest sage?

ESHUORO: Be careful . . . I asked you whether or not today was the day for Aroni's harmless little ceremony. His welcome of the dead. Another mild lesson for those fleas he calls humans. Is it or isn't it?

MURETE: How do I know?

ESHUORO: Don't lie to me. Today is their gathering of the tribes. I know they asked for conquerors and Aroni has sent them accusers, knowing they would never welcome them. So he holds his little feast. A few human witnesses who are returning to their holes, supposedly wiser.

MURETE: Go and complain to Forest Father.

ESHUORO: I was not even invited. Another convenient forgetfulness of Aroni's, isn't it?

MURETE: Don't bring me into your squabbles. They don't interest me.

ESHUORO: Answer quickly. On whose side are you?

MURETE: I hadn't been told we were taking sides.

ESHUORO: Fool. How you survived till now I do not know. Have you seen how they celebrate the gathering of the tribes? In our own destruction. Today they even dared to chase out the forest spirits by poisoning the air with petrol fumes. Have you seen how much of the forest has been torn down for their petty decorations?

MURETE: I know it wasn't the humans who ate my roofing.

[*Eshuoro presses his arm so hard Murete yelps with pain.*]

ESHUORO: Don't talk back, tree gleaner. I'm telling you today must be a day of reprisals. While they are glutted and full of themselves that is the time. Aroni's little ceremony must be made into a bloody sentence. My patience is at an end. Where the humans preserve a little bush behind their homes, it is only because they want somewhere for their garbage. Dead dogs and human excrement are all you'll find in it. The whole forest stinks. Stinks of human obscenities. And who holds us back? Forest Father and his lame minion, Aroni. They and their little ceremonies of gentle rebuke.

MURETE: You feel strongly about it. That is commendable. Isn't Forest Father the one who can help you? Go and talk to him. Or if you are afraid to go, tell me and I'll make you an appointment.

ESHUORO: You had better not go to him if that is in your mind. I'll have you bitten for seven years by ants.

MURETE: Oh. Oh. So you can count on them can you? You have been poisoning the mind of the ants.

ESHUORO: They were not difficult to win over. And they'll be present at the welcoming. Four hundred million of their dead will crush the humans in a load of guilt. Four hundred million callously smoked to death. Since when was the forest so weak that humans could smoke out the owners and sleep after?

MURETE: No one has complained much. We have claimed our own victims—for every tree that is felled or for every beast that is slaughtered, there is recompense, given or forced.

ESHUORO: [*twists his arm.*] Be sure then to take yourself off today. Every one of you that won't come clearly on my side must take himself off. Go into the town if you love them so much and join the gathering of the tribes.

MURETE: What will you do?

ESHUORO: My jester will accompany me. Aroni means to let the humans judge themselves. Good. My jester will teach them how. Aroni means to let them go, afterwards. Means to let them live. Are they not guilty people?

MURETE: Let who go?

ESHUORO: Are you still pretending. The human witnesses he has abducted. He means to let them go afterwards.

MURETE: Eshuoro, you won't dare.

ESHUORO: Not by my hand. But if the humans, as always, wreak havoc on their own heads, who are we to stop them? Don't they always decide their own lives?

MURETE: I am not much concerned. But it seems to me that, limb for limb, the forest has always proved victor.

ESHUORO: This great assemblage of theirs is an affront. And I have suffered the biggest insult any son of Forest Head has ever experienced from the hand of a human insect.

MURETE: Ask for justice from Forest Head.

ESHUORO: Am I his son or am I not? I have told him. I have asked that he pass judgement for my limbs that were hacked off piece by piece. For my eyes that were gouged and my roots disrespectfully made naked to the world. For the desecration of my forest body.

MURETE: What you are talking about? Is it still about the woodcutter who chopped off your top?

ESHUORO: Have you not been to the town centre? Have you not seen this new thing he made for me? The beacon for the gathering of the tribes. Have you not seen the centrepiece of their vulgarity?

URETE: What?

SHUORO: The totem, blind fool, drunk fool, insensitive fool. The totem, my final insult. The final taunt from the human pigs. The tree that is marked down for Oro, the tree from which my follower fell to his death, foully or by accident, I have still to discover when we meet at the next wailing. But my body was stripped by the impious hands of

Demoke, Ogun's favoured slave of the forge. My head was
hacked off by his axe. Trampled, sweated on, bled on, my
body's shame pointed at the sky by the adze of Demoke, will
I let this day pass without vengeance claimed blood for sap?

MURETE: Why... you... mucus off a crab's carbuncle. You
stream of fig pus from the duct of a stumbling bat. That is
an offering which would have gladdened the heart of
Forest Father himself. He would have called it adulation.
Did he not himself teach them the arts, and must they be
confined to little rotted chips which fall off when
Eshuoro peels like a snake of the previous year. Offal of the
hyena tribe, all you want is an excuse to feed on carrion!
Dare you call yourself of the Forest blood? You are only
the greasy recesses of a rodent's nest...

[*Eshuoro breaks a branch off the tree, whirls and whirls it round
him in an effort to smash Murete once for all. Murete runs off.
Eshuoro drops the stick and rages. Does a frenetic jig as he flings
his grievance to the world.*]

ESHUORO: Demoke, son and son to carvers, who taught you
How you impale me, abuse me! Scratching my shame
To the dwellers of hell, where
The womb-snake shudders and the world is set on fire.
Demoke, did you know? Mine is the tallest tree that grows
On land. Mine is the head that cows
The Messengers of heaven. Did you not know?
Demoke, did you not know? Only the tree may eat itself.
Oro alone is the worm that strips himself
Denudes the forest in a night. Only I
May eat the leaves of the silk-cotton tree.
And let men cower and women run to hole.
My voice is thin, my voice is shrill, my voice
Is no child's lullaby to human ears.
Place *mariwo* between your gates and let my knives

Seek the curious eye of the unbidden stranger.
Demoke, watch for the sudden fall of slighted trees
The tallest tree alone is mine, and mine alone.
Skin of my loins, see where it holds the branches.
Where the wind goes, a shred of Oro
Marks the trail, and when it drips, it is not
From camwood dye. Red, red is the colour of the wind
Oro is the nothing that the eye beholds
Spirits of the dead eat and drink of me
Long since the beginning. Spirits of the dead
Have feasted on Oro but do I grow less?
Do I grow thin? Do I cry when the night-bird pecks?
Oro is the nothing that the eye beholds
The child that vanishes and the silent lips of men.
Bathe children of my dead in ram's blood
That I may know them, and spare them
But do not forget the following year, or the year
That comes after; aye, Oro also can forget
And women cry when Oro rubs off yesterdays
Covers with sand the smear of blood proclaiming
That the father rested on the horns of rams.
Demoke, son and son again to pious carvers,
Have you lost fear? Demoke, renegade, beware
The slanted eye of night. Beware
The anger of the silent wind that rustles
Not a leaf. I'll be revenged. Eshuoro, I,
I'll be revenged, I'll be revenged...   [*Rushes out.*]

*

[*Another part of the forest.*
Approaching sound of a gong. Enter the Forest Crier
with a scroll. Strikes his gong. A few Forest Spirits
emerge from hiding places. Mostly, only their faces

can be seen. The Crier walks with a kind of mechanical to and fro movement.]

CRIER: To all such as dwell in these Forests; Rock devils,
Earth imps, Tree demons, ghommids, dewilds, genie
Incubi, succubi, windhorls, bits and halves and such
Sons and subjects of Forest Father, and all
That dwell in his domain, take note, this night
Is the welcome of the dead. When spells are cast
And the dead invoked by the living, only such
May resume their body corporeal as are summoned
When the understreams that whirl them endlessly
Complete a circle. Only such may regain
Voice auditorial as are summoned when their link
With the living has fully repeated its nature, has
Re-impressed fully on the tapestry of Igbehinadun
In approximate duplicate of actions, be they
Of good, or of evil, of violence or carelessness;
In approximate duplicate of motives, be they
Illusory, tangible, commendable or damnable.
Take note, this selection, is by the living.
We hold these rites, at human insistence.
By proclamation, let the mists of generations
Be now dispersed. Forest Father, unveil, unveil
The phantasmagoria of protagonists from the dead.
[*Exit the crier. Forest Father enters, accompanied by Aroni. They remain to one side.*]

FOREST HEAD: Oh, they made amusing companions. It was really their latent violence which frightened me. I did not know what I would do if it involved me.

ARONI: They appear tame enough now.

FOREST HEAD: So tame in fact, I could send them home. But they forget too easily.

ARONI: They had no suspicion of you?

of the Forests

FOREST HEAD: Only uncertainty. I threw dark hints to preserve my mystery and force them into an acceptance of my aloofness. It held them all except the woman.

ARONI: Madame Tortoise.

FOREST HEAD: The same. You have done very well to choose her Aroni. I am very pleased. Ah—Eshuoro?

ARONI: He will find us. I have laid a trail that will bring him to us.

FOREST HEAD: We will make use of him. If the child needs a fright, then the mother must summon the witch. Proverbs to ... How is it spoken by that busy man—Agboreko?

ARONI: [*mimicking.*] Proverb to bones and silence.
[*They laugh.*]

FOREST HEAD: Murete's blood brother is he not? Brother in fermented millet blood. Well, is everything prepared?

ARONI: We are ready.

FOREST HEAD: Remind me, how far back are we?

ARONI: About eight centuries. Possibly more. One of their great empires. I forget which.

FOREST HEAD: It matters nothing ...

[*Aroni waves his hand in a circle. The court of Mata Kharibu lights up gradually. Two thrones. One contains Mata Kharibu, the other, his queen, Madame Tortoise, both surrounded by splendour. A page plucks an African guitar. Mata Kharibu is angry; his eyes roll terribly; the court cowers. His queen, on the other hand, is very gay and cruel in her coquetry. She seems quite oblivious of the king's condition. The court poet (Demoke) stands a few feet from her. Behind him stands his scribe, a young boy, pen and scroll at the ready. Those not involved in the action at any time, freeze in one position.*]

MADAME TORTOISE: [*gaily.*] I am sad.

COURT POET: It is a mantle, my lady, woven only for the gracious. Sadness is noble my lady, and you wear it like the night. [*Aside.*] And I hope it smothers you like one.

MADAME TORTOISE: The sadness will not leave me. I have lost my canary.

COURT POET: Your canary, Madame? Would you say—and I do wish it Madame—that you had lost your head?

MADAME TORTOISE: Unriddle me.

COURT POET: My lady, I would not say, look up. It is not given to the eye to perceive its own beauty. Reflection is nothing, except in the eye of a sensitive soul. Mirror is dross.

MADAME TORTOISE: [*gaily.*] I am impatient.

COURT POET: Your hair is the feathers my lady, and the breast of the canary—your forehead my lady—is the inspiration of your servant. Madame, you must not say you have lost your canary—[*aside*] unless it also be your virtue, slut!

MADAME TORTOISE: And yet I would have it here, with me. Can you fly as high with your feet as you conjure so easily with words?

COURT POET: Madame, it is my turn to be unriddled.

MADAME TORTOISE: I know where my canary is, but will you fetch it for me. I want it here with me.

COURT POET: Command me, my lady!

MADAME TORTOISE: On the roof-top. Fetch it, poet.

COURT POET: [*leans out of a window. Whistles.*]

MADAME TORTOISE: No fool. Do you want it to tire itself with flying?

COURT POET: My lady, you were born on satin, on brocades and red velvet. A canary, was born on wings.

MADAME TORTOISE: Go after it. The canary will like you better for it.

[*The poet's novice quickly lays down his scroll.*]

NOVICE: Indeed, a royal bird may not be tired. And my hands are soft. I will fetch the canary.

MADAME TORTOISE: If your tutor gives permission, certainly. What do you say, my poet?

of the Forests

COURT POET: Did not a soldier fall to his death from the roof two days ago my lady?

MADAME TORTOISE: That is so. I heard a disturbance, and I called the guard to find the cause. I thought it came from the roof and I directed him there. He was too eager and he fell.

COURT POET: From favour Madame?

MADAME TORTOISE: [*eyeing him coolly.*] From the roof.
[*They look at each other.*]

MADAME TORTOISE: Well?

COURT POET: I forbid him to go.

MADAME TORTOISE: I order him to go.
[*The novice runs off.*]

MADAME TORTOISE: And I order you to follow him. When he has retrieved my canary, bring it here to me, like a servant.
[*The poet bows and leaves. Madame Tortoise and her attendants remain statuesque.*]
[*From the opposite side, a warrior is pushed in, feet chained together. Mata Kharibu leaps up at once. The warrior is the Dead Man. He is still in his warrior garb, only it is bright and new.*]

MATA KHARIBU: [*advancing slowly on him.*] It was you, slave! You it was who dared to think.

WARRIOR: I plead guilty to the possession of thought. I did not know that it was in me to exercise it, until your Majesty's inhuman commands.
[*Mata Kharibu slaps him across the face.*]

MATA KHARIBU: You have not even begun to repent of your madness.

WARRIOR: Madness your Majesty?

MATA KHARIBU: Madness! Treachery! Frothing insanity traitor! Do you dare to question my words?

WARRIOR: No, terrible one. Only your commands.
[*Mata Kharibu whips out his sword. Raises it. The soldier bows his head.*]

PHYSICIAN: Your Majesty! [*He hurries forward. Whispers in Kharibu's ear. Kharibu subsides, goes back to his throne, and watches them, glowering.*] You know me. You know you can trust me.

WARRIOR: I know you are in the pay of Mata Kharibu.

PHYSICIAN: But you cannot accuse me of inhumanity. I saved you twice from being tortured. And just now I saved your life. Try and think of me only as a friend.
[*The soldier remains silent.*]
I am trying to help you. Not only you, but your men who regard you so much as their leader that they can refuse to fight when you order them not to.

WARRIOR: It is an unjust war. I cannot lead my men into battle merely to recover the trousseau of any woman.

PHYSICIAN: Ah. But do you not see? It goes further than that. It is no longer the war of the queen's wardrobe. The war is now an affair of honour.

WARRIOR: An affair of honour? Since when was it an honourable thing to steal the wife of a brother chieftain?

PHYSICIAN: Can you really judge the action of another?

WARRIOR: No. But the results, and when they affect me and men who place their trust in me. If the king steals another's wife, it is his affair. But let it remain so. Mata Kharibu thought, hoped that the dishonoured king would go to war on her account. There he was wrong. It seems her rightful husband does not consider that your new queen is worth a battle. But Mata Kharibu is so bent on bloodshed that he sends him a new message. Release the goods of this woman I took from you if there will be peace between us. Is this the action of a ruler who values the peace of his subjects?

PHYSICIAN: A man cannot take a wife without a dowry. Mata Kharibu asks what is rightly his. The dowry of a woman he takes to wife.

WARRIOR: I understand. I thank you for enlightening me, Physician.

PHYSICIAN: And will you fight?

WARRIOR: You have done your work. You may tell the king that I was mad before, but now I am fully returned to my senses.

[*The Physician looks at him doubtfully.*]

Go to him sir. Or perhaps I ought to say, go and make your report to the woman who now rules all our lives— even Mata Kharibu. Go to the woman who draws the frown on his face and greases the thunder of his voice. Tell her I know her ambitions. I will not fight her war.

PHYSICIAN: Fool. A soldier does not choose his wars.

WARRIOR: Is Mata Kharibu not a soldier?

PHYSICIAN: Was ever a man so bent on his own destruction!

WARRIOR: If that referred to the king, you have spoken your first true word today.

PHYSICIAN: Future generations will label you traitor. Your son, your children will all call you . . . a-ah I remember now. You have a wife have you not? An expectant mother?

WARRIOR: I know what runs in your head. But it will not help you. Summon the tears of my wife and her unborn child if you so desire. But there is no leader who will not feel a stronger tie of blood with soldiers than with a stranger he took to wife. My duty is to my men.

[*The Physician shuffles, uncertain how to proceed.*]

PHYSICIAN: Unborn generations will . . .

WARRIOR: Unborn generations will be cannibals most worshipful Physician. Unborn generations will, as we have done, eat up one another. Perhaps you can devise a cure, you who know how to cure so many ills. I took up soldiering to defend my country, but those to whom I gave the power to command my life abuse my trust in them.

PHYSICIAN: Liar! Is Mata Kharibu not your general!

WARRIOR: Mata Kharibu is leader, not merely of soldiers but of men. Let him turn the unnatural pattern of men always eating up one another. I am suddenly weary of this soldiering where men must find new squabbles for their cruelty. Must I tell the widowed that their men died for another's trousseau?

PHYSICIAN: You think your own life is yours to dispose of?

WARRIOR: I have the right to choose how I mean to die.

PHYSICIAN: Your own life. Are you sure that no one else may waste your life except you?

WARRIOR: Why do you continue this useless questioning? I have told you that I am ready to submit my neck to...

PHYSICIAN: But the others... the others... Have you a right to submit the neck of another?

WARRIOR: What do you mean?

PHYSICIAN: Your men. The soldiers who follow you. The men you have misled. They have become traitors like you or do you not know that?

WARRIOR: They made their choice themselves. They must do as they decide.

PHYSICIAN: You have told them what to think. You have ordered their feelings. These men are used to obeying you. If you are so determined to die, you must first release them of their allegiance to you.

WARRIOR: [*looks up. Breaks into a smile.*] I see. Now I understand what you want. You are afraid. Mata Kharibu is afraid.

PHYSICIAN: [*scared.*] Be quiet. For heaven's sake do not speak so loud.

of the Forests

WARRIOR: But I am right. Perhaps I have started a new disease that catches quickly.

[*Enter the Historian (Adenebi) with scrolls.*]

HISTORIAN: Don't flatter yourself. Every blade of grass that has allowed its own contamination can be burnt out. This thing cannot last. It is unheard of. In a thousand years it will be unheard of. Nations live by strength; nothing else has meaning. You only throw your life away uselessly.

MATA KHARIBU: [*apprehensive.*] Did you find anything?

HISTORIAN: There is no precedent, your Highness.

MATA KHARIBU: You have looked thoroughly?

HISTORIAN: It is unheard of. War is the only consistency that past ages afford us. It is the legacy which new nations seek to perpetuate. Patriots are grateful for wars. Soldiers have never questioned bloodshed. The cause is always the accident your Majesty, and war is the Destiny. This man is a traitor. He must be in the enemy's pay.

MATA KHARIBU: He has taken sixty of my best soldiers with him.

HISTORIAN: Your Highness has been too lenient. Is the nation to ignore the challenge of greatness because of the petty-mindedness of a few cowards and traitors.

WARRIOR: I am no traitor!

HISTORIAN: Be quiet Soldier! I have here the whole history of Troy. If you were not the swillage of pigs and could read the writings of wiser men, I would show you the magnificence of the destruction of a beautiful city. I would reveal to you the attainments of men which lifted mankind to the ranks of gods and demi-gods. And who was the inspiration of this divine carnage? Helen of Troy, a woman whose honour became as rare a conception as her beauty. Would Troy, if it were standing today lay claim to preservation in the annals of history if a thousand valiant Greeks had not been slaughtered before its gates, and a hundred thousand Trojans within her walls? Do you, a mere cog in the wheel of Destiny, cover your face and whine like a thing that is unfit to lick a soldier's boots, you, a Captain . . . Your Majesty, I am only the Court historian and I crave your august indulgence for any excess of zeal. But history has always revealed that the soldier who will not fight has the blood of slaves in him. For the sake of your humble subjects, this renegade must be treated as a slave.

MATA KHARIBU: Not only he. Every one who thinks like him, be he soldier or merchant. I will have no moral termites a thousand miles within my domain. Mata Kharibu is not the idle eye that watches contemptible insects eat away the strength of his kindgom.

[*The Soothsayer (Agboreko) enters.*]

MATA KHARIBU: If you come to tell me of unfavourable stars, soothsayer, turn round and go out again. We will fight this war in spite of cowards or auguries.

SOOTHSAYER: I see much blood Mata Kharibu. On both sides of the plough.

MATA KHARIBU: I will be satisfied with that. Does it not mean a great battle? On Kharibu's side at least, there will be real soldiers fighting. Sell that man down the river. He and his men. Sell them all down the river.

PHYSICIAN: Think again your Highness. It is a whole company.

HISTORIAN: His Majesty has decided wisely. Those men can never again be trusted.

MATA KHARIBU: I want them taken away immediately. I do not want sight or smell of them after sunset. If no boat can be found, drown them.

SLAVE-DEALER: Your Majesty!

MATA KHARIBU: I will hear no petitions today.

SLAVE-DEALER: [*throwing himself forward.*] I am no petitioner

of the Forests

Mata Kharibu. I merely place my vessel at the disposal of your august Majesty.

MATA KHARIBU: Oh! you. Are you not the slave-dealer?

SLAVE-DEALER: Your humble servant is amply rewarded. Your Highness has deigned before to use me as an agent, and hearing that there was to be another war, I came to offer my services. However, if there are slaves even before the battle has begun ...

MATA KHARIBU: They are yours. If they are out of my Kingdom before an hour, I shall not forget you.

PHYSICIAN: Mata Kharibu, most humane of monarchs, the crime of your soldiers is a terrible one, but do not place men who once served you faithfully in the hands of that merchant.

MATA KHARIBU: Why? What is this?

PHYSICIAN: Sir, I know the man of old, and I know the slight coffin in which he stuffs his victims. He knows how to get them down alive; it is his trade. But until he is near the slave-market, the wretches have gone through the twenty torments of hell.

SLAVE-DEALER: I have a new vessel. A true palace worthy of renegade soldiers. You malign me Physician?

HISTORIAN: Mata Kharibu need not be troubled about their fate. Their lives are forfeit.

PHYSICIAN: Then execute them at once your Highness. Kill them all but do not deliver them into his hands.

SLAVE-DEALER: Come down to the shore and into my vessel, and I will not ask you before you strip your body and lie contented as ...

PHYSICIAN: Don't try your oily words with me, liar!

SLAVE-DEALER: But I assure you Mr. Physician ...

MATA KHARIBU: Silence! Have I now become the market overseer that you squabble before me which stick drives the cattle to the sale? Beware lest the blood that is let at the battle be nothing compared to the heads that will roll if one more voice forgets to lower itself in my hearing. Villains! Has the rot that has beset my soldiers already spread into my court that I cannot even think because a bazaar has been opened before my throne!

[*He storms off. He is about to pass by the Soothsayer when he stops, pulls him aside.*]

MATA KHARIBU: I saw it on your face. The stars were unfavourable?

SOOTHSAYER: Then why do you proceed?

MATA KHARIBU: It is too late to stop. I have been frightened. I dare not stop. I cannot stop. That captain of my army has put a curse on me.

SOOTHSAYER: A curse? Then that may explain...

MATA KHARIBU: No. Not like that. They have not cursed me as you think. But this new thing... You are wise. Surely you can understand. It is unheard of. I shall be shamed before generations to come. What does it mean? Why should my slave, my subject, my mere human property say, unless he is mad, I shall not fight this war. Is he a freak?

SOOTHSAYER: No.

MATA KHARIBU: I could understand it if he aimed at my throne. But he is not even man for that. What does it mean? What do you see for me in the future? Will there be more like him, born with this thought cancer in their heart?

SOOTHSAYER: Mata Kharibu, have you ever seen a smudge on the face of the moon?

MATA KHARIBU: What do you mean?

SOOTHSAYER: Have you?

MATA KHARIBU: No.

SOOTHSAYER: And yet it happens. Once in every million years, one of the sheep that trail the moon in its wanderings does dare to wipe its smutty nose on the moon. Once in a million years. But the moon is there still. And who remembers the envy-ridden sheep?

MATA KHARIBU: So the future holds nothing for men like him?

SOOTHSAYER: Nothing. Nothing at all.

MATA KHARIBU: [*going.*] At least, in the reign of Mata Kharibu, I shall see that your words are true.

SOOTHSAYER: [*looking after him, musingly.*] No. It does not depend on you, Mata Kharibu. It is in the nature of men to seek power over the lives of others, and there is always something lower than a servant. [*Goes.*]

[*During the foregoing, the Slave-dealer and the Historian exchange furtive whispers. As soon as Mata Kharibu leaves the court, the Physician marches purposefully towards the Slave-dealer.*]

PHYSICIAN: You shifty, miserable flesh merchant, how dare you suggest that you have the space in that finger-bowl to transport sixty full-grown men?

SLAVE-DEALER: Honourable Physician to the court of Mata Kharibu, why this concern for the health of traitors condemned to a fate worse than death?

PHYSICIAN: Mata Kharibu is not so devoid of humanity as to ...

SLAVE-DEALER: I have no wish to argue that point. Mr. Physician, I assure you most sincerely that you are mistaken. My new vessel is capable of transporting the whole of Kharibu's court to hell—when that time does come. The Honourable Historian here can testify to it. I took him aboard ...
[*Behind his back, he passes a bag of money to the Historian, who takes it, feels it and pockets it.*] ... only this afternoon, and showed him every plank and rope ... ask him yourself.

HISTORIAN: That is a fact. Mata Kharibu and all his ancestors would be proud to ride in such a boat.

PHYSICIAN: In that case ... I ...

SLAVE-DEALER: I take my leave of you. Be good enough to give me your official clearance. I have only an hour, remember. [*Goes.*]

HISTORIAN: Do come for some sherbet at my house . . . [*places his arm round the Physician.*] . . . You are a learned man and I would appreciate an opportunity to discuss the historical implications of this . . . mutiny . . . if one can really call it that . . . We were so near to the greatness of Troy and Greece . . . I mean this is war as it should be fought . . . over nothing . . . do you not agree?

[*They go off.*]

[*The Court Poet enters with a golden cage, containing a canary.*]

MADAME TORTOISE: You were late returning, poet.

COURT POET: Such is the generosity of my lady's smiles, the poet is now indulged, and cannot abide storms. Madame, I waited until sunshine was restored—[*aside*] hoping it would shrivel you.

MADAME TORTOISE: Is that my canary? I no longer desire it.

COURT POET: It is the privilege of Beauty to be capricious.

MADAME TORTOISE: You return alone. Where is your novice?

COURT POET: My pupil Madame? He was so eager to earn the good graces of your Highness.

MADAME TORTOISE: And may no one deserve them but you?

COURT POET: No one, your Highness. No one else.

MADAME TORTOISE: You have not told me. Where is your pupil?

COURT POET: Being a good pupil Madame, he has just learned a new lesson.

MADAME TORTOISE: I am waiting to learn too, poet. What lesson was this?

COURT POET: In short Madame, he was too eager, and he fell.

MADAME TORTOISE: How fell? What do you mean? Is he dead?

COURT POET: No Madame. Only a mild fall. He broke an arm.

[*They stare each other in the eye.*]

MADAME TORTOISE: So, so.

COURT POET: That roof is dangerous Madame. Did not a soldier also fall from the same spot?

MADAME TORTOISE: [*mocking.*] He was too eager, and he fell.
[*Again, they look each other in the eye.*]

COURT POET: So, so, your Highness...

MADAME TORTOISE: Leave me now poet. And take the bird with you. And look out my poet; sometimes, you grow wearisome.
[*Court Poet bows, and departs. The queen looks around. Eyes the kneeling soldier for a few moments, then claps her hands. The Court is instantly cleared, except for the soldier and his guard. She angrily signals the guard off and he disappears.*]

MADAME TORTOISE: Come here soldier.
[*When there is still no response, she smiles, and rises voluptuously. Stands very close to the soldier.*]

MADAME TORTOISE: [*jerks up his head suddenly, laughing.*] You are the one that will not fight for me?

WARRIOR: Madame, I beg you to keep your distance. Restraint is a difficult exercise for a man condemned to dishonour.

MADAME TORTOISE: Restraint ha! That is a virtue lacked by your soldiers... or did you not know that?

WARRIOR: I did not mean that kind of restraint. Madame, I know what havoc you have wreaked among my men, and we now face the final destruction of a good band of loyal men. Somehow, I do not hate you. But I do know the power of blood on the brain. I beg you to keep beyond my hands.

MADAME TORTOISE: [*thrusts herself quite close to him.*] A man. You speak like a man. No wonder your men are all men, every one of them. They have been well taught by their leader. It is a marvellous thing. These men were stupid, but they come under a leader, a man, and suddenly they stand upright and demand more than what is theirs. I did not know until now that you spoke through them all.

WARRIOR: Madame, desist from this torture.

MADAME TORTOISE: Torture! I have cause to torture you. Did you know the one who fell from the roof? The one who leapt to his death, on my account?

WARRIOR: Madame!

MADAME TORTOISE: He could not understand that I took him, just as I select a new pin every day. He came back again and could not understand why the door was barred to him. He was such a fool.

WARRIOR: I have no wish to hear.

MADAME TORTOISE: Your soldiers gave me my name. It is one I revel in. You may call me by that name.

[*The soldier shuts his eyes fiercely, tries to stop his ears but his hands are chained together.*]

MADAME TORTOISE: Mata Kharibu is a fool. You are a man and a leader, Soldier. Have you no wish to sit where Mata Kharibu sits?

WARRIOR: I cannot hear you Madame, I cannot hear you!

MADAME TORTOISE: Call me by my name. Madame Tortoise. I am the one who outlasts you all. Madame Tortoise. You are a man, I swear I must respect you.

WARRIOR: Guard! Guard!

MADAME TORTOISE: I can save you. I can save you alone, or with your men. Choose. Choose. Why should a man be wasted? Why must you waste yourself for a fool like Kharibu? Choose, and let me be with you.

SOLDIER: Guard! Guard!

MADAME TORTOISE: What are you? Men have killed for me. Men have died for me. Have you flints in your eye? Fool, have you never lived?

WARRIOR: [*desperately.*] Guard!

[*A woman, dishevelled, rushes in, followed by a guard, who clutches her shawl. They come to a stop as the queen turns on them, face contorted with fury. The woman is pregnant. (She is the Dead Woman.)*]

WARRIOR: [*turning slowly, nearly breaking down.*] Go home, in heaven's name, go home.

MADAME TORTOISE: [*her face breaks into fiendishness.*] I knew it was incredible. It could not be. I, Madame Tortoise, spurned by a common soldier. For that! Was it for that?

[*The wife moves towards the queen, falls on her knees.*]

WOMAN: [*very faintly.*] Mercy!

MADAME TORTOISE: Guard. Pay close attention to my words. Do eunuchs not fetch a good price at the market?

GUARD: Madame?

WOMAN: Have pity. Have pity.

MADAME TORTOISE: [*to the Warrior.*] You are lost. But have your wish. Warriors are sold as men but eunuchs guard the harems of other Mata Kharibus, drooling on wares that they cannot taste. Choose!

[*The Captain looks at his wife, who turns her face to the ground.*]

MADAME TORTOISE: I am impatient. I will not be trifled with!

[*The Captain continues to look at his wife.*]

MADAME TORTOISE: Guard. You know my sentence. See that you carry it out.

[*The woman clasps her womb, gasps and collapses. Sudden black-out. Immediate light to reveal Aroni and Forest Head, who continue to stare into the spectacle. They remain so for several moments.*]

ESHUORO: [*striding in, with his jester at his heels.*] The soldier was a fool.

ARONI: Eshuoro!

ESHUORO: The soldier was a fool. A woman. He was a woman. What have you proved?

ARONI: I see you could not be kept away.

ESHUORO: I was not invited. Once again, I was marked down to be slighted. Aroni, I warn you beware. You walk close to the Father of Forests and I suspect you do me an ill turn at every word.

FOREST HEAD: Be silent then and do not harm yourself with your every word.

ESHUORO: When is the gentle admonishment? The spectacle is over and not a word of the ills wreaked on me. Have I not lodged complaint? I hear no word of redress. I have been assaulted and my follower murdered—yes, I know it now—murdered. Must I be minced and ground in the dust before Forest Head deigns to look my way?

FOREST HEAD: I forget nothing. There is still the welcome of the dead. I omit nothing.

[*Enter Ogun.*]

OGUN: Face to face at last Eshuoro. Do you come here with your loud words and empty boasts? Soulless one, Demoke is no empty nut that fell, motherless from the sky. In all that he did, he followed my bidding. I will speak for him.

ESHUORO: I have suffered this too long. Perhaps the master must first be taught and then he can teach his minions to be humble.

OGUN: Minion? This minion of mine Eshuoro—is it not rumoured that he has done you service lately as a barber?

ESHUORO: [*between his teeth.*] I have borne too much already to take your taunts lightly. Ogun, I warn you beware ...

OGUN: Eshuoro, what news of Oremole?

ESHUORO: Take care ...

OGUN: What news of Oremole, slave to my servant. Did you sleep when your butcher frightened earth with his screams and his legs opened foolishly on his downward way to hell?

of the Forests

ESHUORO: You can hear him. Do you all bear with this against me?

OGUN: You look shaven on the skull Eshuoro. And I think once, there were more hairs on your chest. Have not I seen you at the gathering of the tribes, wet and naked by my servants' hands?

[*Eshuoro takes a sudden leap at him. Thunderclap. Black-out. Forest Head is next seen holding them apart, without touching them.*]

FOREST HEAD: Soon, I will not tell you from the humans, so closely have their habits grown on you. Did I summon this welcoming for your prowess or for ends of my own? Take care how you tempt my vanity. Eshuoro, you came here to bathe in blood, Ogun, you to defend the foibles of your ward. Let this night alone, when I lay out the rites of the dead or my anger will surpass your spleen. Aroni, you know my will. Proceed.

ESHUORO: What will you achieve?

ARONI: It is enough that they discover their own regeneration.

ESHUORO: Another trick. I came here for vengeance.

FOREST HEAD: I know.

ESHUORO: And I will not leave without it.

ARONI: You have your case. Let the future judge them by reversal of its path or by stubborn continuation.

OGUN: Will you forsee the many confusions Eshuoro hatches in his mind? Aroni, let my servant go. He has suffered enough.

ARONI: I need him most of all.

OGUN: He has no guilt. I, Ogun, swear that his hands were mine in every action of his life.

FOREST HEAD: Will you all never rid yourselves of these conceits!

ESHUORO: I am impatient.

ARONI: You must wait, like us. In any case the Forest Spirits have gone to the gathering of the tribes. Or did you not know that—Eshuoro?

ESHUORO: And so the future will not be chorused. I know it. I have seen through your tricks of delay.

ARONI: I said you must wait. Forest Head has provided for the default of your brothers. The living ones will themselves speak for the future. For the event, they will be, like you, of the Forest. Have you a better suggestion, brother fiend?

ESHUORO: [*slowly.*] Why? Why are you so ready with a solution?

FOREST HEAD: Was it not the same remedy with which you boldly and with confidence approached us? Was it not to this end that you frightened away all those who would not attend the welcome to speak on your behalf? Since when was I smitten with deafness or blindness, Eshuoro?

ESHUORO: I threatened none.

FOREST HEAD: Enough. Do not deny that all goes as you planned it. [*Eshuoro goes out.*] But only because it is my wish. And so we all must be content. Call the questioner and let no one foully intervene for the furthering of his cause.
[*Back-scene lights up gradually to reveal a dark, wet, atmosphere dripping moisture, and soft, moist soil. A palm-tree sways at a low angle, broken but still alive. Seemingly lightning-reduced stumps. Rotting wood all over the ground. A mound or two here and there. Footfalls are muffled. First, there is total stillness, emphasized by the sound of moisture dripping to the ground. Forest Head is sitting on a large stone, statuesque, the Questioner stands beside him. Aroni is no longer to be seen. The Dead Woman enters, dead as on first appearance. She behaves exactly as before, hesitant, seemingly lost.*]

QUESTIONER: Who sent you?

DEAD WOMAN: I am certain she had no womb, but I think
It was a woman.

QUESTIONER: Before your time?
Was it before your time?

DEAD WOMAN: I have come to ask that of
    The knowing ones. My knowledge is
    The hate alone. The little ball of hate
    Alone consumed me. Wet runnels
    Of the earth brought me hither.
    Call Forest Head. Say someone comes
    For all the rest. Say someone asks—
    Was it for this, for this,
    Children plagued their mothers?

QUESTIONER: A mother, and in haste?
    Were there no men? No barren women,
    Aged and toothless women?
    What called you forth beyond the backyard fence?
    Beyond the cooking pots? What made you deaf
    To the life that begged within you?
    Had he no claim?

DEAD WOMAN: For him. It was for him.

QUESTIONER: You should have lived for him. Did you dare
    Snatch death from those that gasped for breath?

DEAD WOMAN: My weakness, Forest Head. I was a woman
    I was weak.

QUESTIONER: And the other. The one who sent you.
    The one you call a wombless woman
    Was she weak?
    [*The woman is silent.*]

FOREST HEAD: Every day. Every hour. Where will it end?
    Child, there is no choice but one of suffering
    And those who tread the understreams
    Add ashes to the hairs
    Of Forest Father. Rest awhile.
    The beings of the Forest have been called
    To dance the welcome, to quiet your spirit
    Torn loosely by the suddenness. And roots

Have brought us news of another son
And he has come a longer way, almost
They murmur, from quite another world.
[*The Dead Man, after a still silence, enters.*]

DEAD MAN: Three lives I led since first I went away
But still my first possesses me
The pattern is unchanged.

QUESTIONER: You who enter sleek and well fed
Have you, at least, a tale of
Pleasure and content?

DEAD MAN: My father said, and his great father
Before him, if you find no rest, go home
And they will know you.
Kind friends, take me to Forest Head.

FOREST HEAD: I knew you, Mulieru . . .

DEAD MAN: Then you are Forest Head. When I died
And still they would not let my body rest;
When I lived, and they would not let me be
The man I felt, cutting my manhood, first
With a knife, next with words and the dark
Spit of contempt, the voice at my shoulder said,
Go seek out Forest Head. If I am home, then
I have come to sleep.

QUESTIONER: When the fattened calf complains of hunger
May one not fear his brain is seized
With fever?

FOREST HEAD: Hush! Mulieru, I knew you
In the days of pillaging, in the days
Of sudden slaughter, and the parting
Of child and brother. I knew you
In the days of grand destroying
And you a part of the waste.
Mulieru, you were one of those who journeyed

of the Forests

       In the market-ships of blood.
       You were sold Mulieru, for ...
QUESTIONER: [*who has been consulting his barks.*] ... a flask of rum.
DEAD MAN: Then I am home
    If it was I Mulieru, who
    Rowed the slave-ship to the beating
    Of the lash, the sea has paid its debt.
QUESTIONER: Your wise men, casting bones of oracle
    Promised peace and profit
    New knowledge, new beginnings after toil
    Mulieru, sleek and fat, and skin-mellowed Mulieru
    Was there not fruit and corn-wine at the end?
DEAD MAN: Flesh there is upon my bones
    As the skin is flesh-filled on the bones
    Of every gelded pig.
    [*The Questioner approaches, touches him, presses his skin and withdraws his hand in sudden disgust, wiping it on the soil.*]
QUESTIONER: Three hundred rings have formed
    Three hundred rings within that bole
    Since Mulieru went away, was sold away
    And the tribe was scattered
    Three hundred moultings of
    The womb-snake of the world
    And does the son return now
    Empty-handed?
FOREST HEAD: Enough. Enough.
    The priest was burnt, and do you ask
    What became of his beard?
QUESTIONER: Three lives he boasted of, and each
    A certain waste, foolishly cast aside.
    Has he learnt the crime of laziness?
    What did he prove, from the first when,
    Power at his grasp, he easily

Surrendered his manhood. It was surely
The action of a fool. What did he prove?
And does he come whining here for sleep?
Let him wander a hundred further...
[*Enter Aroni, looking puzzled.*
Reaches suddenly and rips off the Questioner's mask. It is
Eshuoro, and he immediately rushes off. There is only
amusement on the face of Forest Head.]

ARONI: I was sure I recognized a similarity in venom, but I did not think even Eshuoro would dare.

OGUN: [*entering.*] For my part I have played fairly.

FOREST HEAD: I know it. Nothing is affected. But where is my Questioner? No, it matters no longer. It is time we had the welcome. Let the earthly protagonists be called, and see that the Interpreter is present.

[*Low music of Ibo flutes in the background. Enter the*
Interpreter leading Demoke, Rola, Adenebi, resignation on each
face as they were last seen following Obaneji.]

Let the one whose incompletion denies him rest be patient till the Forest has chorused the Future through lips of earth-beings.

[*At this, the Dead Man makes a dumb distressed protest, but*
Aroni leads him off.
Forest Head subjects the Interpreter to severe scrutiny.]

FOREST HEAD: [*eventually.*] You are not the Interpreter I knew.

INTERPRETER: Like the others, he went to...

FOREST HEAD: The gathering of the tribes, do I not know it?

INTERPRETER: I am his acolyte. I shall do my best.

FOREST HEAD: Note that I have my eyes on you. If Eshuoro sent you...

[*Eshuoro enters, sulkily.*]

ESHUORO: Eshuoro needs no slaves to fulfil his designs.

FOREST HEAD: Then mind you do not do your own slaving—at

of the Forests

my bidding. I am the rock of patience, but my bosom is hard.
[*Re-enter Aroni.*]

FOREST HEAD: Aroni, relieve this woman of her burden and let the tongue of the unborn, stilled for generations, be loosened.

[*Dead Woman is led off by Aroni.
Soft rhythmic drumming accompanies Forest Head's last instruction. The Interpreter moves and masks the three protagonists. The mask-motif is as their state of mind—resigned passivity. Once masked, each begins to move round in a slowly widening circle, but they stop to speak, and resume their sedate pace as they chorus the last words.*]

FOREST HEAD: [*When the three are masked.*]
I take no part, but listen. If shadows,
Future shadows form in rain-water
Held in hollow leaves, this is the moment
For the welcome of the dead.

[*Goes to his seat, impassive.
Enter the Dead Woman, unpregnant, leading the Half-Child by the hand. As each spirit is summoned, one of the human three becomes agitated, possessed and then pronounces.*]

INTERPRETER: [*calls.*] Spirit of the Palm!

SPIRIT OF THE PALM: White skeins wove me, I, Spirit of the Palm
Now course I red.
I who suckle blackened hearts, know
Heads will fall down,
Crimson in their bed!

[*The Half-Child, startled, tries to find out which of them it was that spoke. Failing, he lets go of the Dead Woman's hand, leaves her side. A Figure in Red appears, and begins to walk deliberately in his footprints. The Half-Child crosses to the opposite side, digs a little hole in the ground, and begins to play a game of 'sesan'. He has no sooner flicked the first seed than the Figure in Red squats behind him and leans over to join in the game. The Half-Child immediately gets up, the Figure in Red following. The Half-Child seems to appeal for help mutely from those around him, but they stand silent. The Figure in Red keeps close behind him. Downcast, the Half-Child returns to his game, speaking as he goes.]*

HALF-CHILD: I who yet await a mother
Feel this dread,
Feel this dread,
I who flee from womb
To branded womb, cry it now
I'll be born dead
I'll be born dead.

INTERPRETER: Spirit of the Dark!

SPIRIT OF DARKNESS: More have I seen, I, Spirit of the Dark,
Naked they breathe within me, foretelling now
How, by the dark of peat and forest
They'll be misled
And the shutters of the leaves
Shall close down on the doomed
And naked head.

HALF-CHILD: [*softly, without detracting from the intensity of his game.*]
Branded womb, branded womb...

SPIRIT OF THE PALM: White skeins wove me.

SPIRIT OF DARKNESS: Peat and forest.

INTERPRETER: Spirit of Precious Stones!

SPIRIT OF PRECIOUS STONES: Still do I draw them, down
Into the pit that glitters, I
Spirit of gold and diamonds
Mine is the vain light courting death
A-ah! Blight this eye that threaded
Rocks with light, earth with golden lodes
Traitor to the guardian tribe, turn
Turn to lead!

of the Forests

HALF-CHILD: Branded womb, branded womb.
SPIRIT OF THE PALM: White skeins wove me.
SPIRIT OF DARKNESS: Peat and forest.
SPIRIT OF PRECIOUS STONES: Courting death.
INTERPRETER: The Pachyderms!
SPIRIT OF THE PACHYDERMS: Blood that rules the sunset, bathe
    This, our ivory red
    Broken is the sleep of giants
    Wanton raiders, ivory has a point
    Thus, thus we bled.
HALF-CHILD: Branded womb, branded womb.
SPIRIT OF THE PALM: White skeins wove me.
SPIRIT OF DARKNESS: Peat and forest.
SPIRIT OF PRECIOUS STONES: Courting death.
SPIRIT OF THE PACHYDERMS: Thus we bled.
INTERPRETER: Spirit of the Rivers!
SPIRIT OF THE RIVERS: From Limpopo to the Nile coils but one snake
    On mudbanks, and sandy bed
    I who mock the deserts, shed a tear
    Of pity to form palm-ringed oases
    Stain my bowels red!
[*Silence. All movement stops except for the Half-Child and the Figure in Red playing out their game. The Figure in Red flicks all the seeds into the hole, the Half-Child scoring none. Triumphantly he scoops up the seeds in his hand, rises fully. Forest Head rises, Aroni with him. There is some measure of consternation from the forest spirits. He looks round to where Eshuoro was last seen. Eshuoro is no longer there. Aroni makes a move towards the Figure in Red, but Forest Head restrains him. From a distance, a slow rumble, gathering force.*]
CHORUS OF THE WATERS: Let no man then lave his feet
    In any stream, in any lake

In rapids or in cataracts
Let no woman think to bake
Her cornmeal wrapped in leaves
With water gathered of the rain
He'll think his eye deceives
Who treads the ripples where I run
In shallows. The stones shall seem
As kernels, his the presser's feet
Standing in the rich, and red, and cloying stream . . .

SPIRIT OF THE RIVERS: Then shall men say that I the Mother
Have joined veins with the Palm my Brother.

CHORUS OF THE WATERS: Let the Camel mend his leaking hump
Let the squirrel guard the hollows in the Stump.

[*The distant noise grows more insistent. What appears to be a cloud of dust begins to rise steadily, darkening the scene. Aroni moves with sudden determination towards the Figure in Red, but the Interpreter begins a sudden dance which comes between them, and Aroni is forced to retreat.*]

INTERPRETER: Spirit of the Sun! Spirit of the Sun!

SPIRIT OF THE SUN: Red is the pit of the sun's entrails, and I
Who light the crannies of the bole
Would speak, but shadows veil the eye
That pierces with the thorn. I know the stole
That warms the shoulders of the moon.
But this is not its shadow. And I trace
No course that leaves a cloud. The Sun cries Noon
Whose hand is it that covers up his face!

[*The forest spirits murmur together on one side, Aroni and Forest Head confer on the other.*]

FOREST HEAD: Who are you?
Why do you blanket earth and swarm
Like molten rocks?

SPIRIT OF VOLCANOES: Nipples I engender, scattered

>   Through the broad breast of the earth,
>   I, Spirit of erupting mountains
>   But I am not now winded. I have not belched
>   These twenty hours or more. I have spat
>   No hot ashes in the air.
> FOREST HEAD: If the hills are silent, who are these,
>   If the sun is full and the winds are still
>   Whose hand is this that reaches from the grave?
> ANT LEADER: We take our colour from the loam
>   And blindness hits them, and they tread us
>   Underfoot.
> FOREST HEAD: Are you my sons?
> ANT LEADER: We are the blazers of the trail
>   If you are Forest Father, we think
>   We are your sons.
> FOREST HEAD: But who are you?
> ANT LEADER: We take our colour from the fertile loam
>   Our numbers from the hair-roots of the earth
>   And terror blinds them. They know
>   We are the children of earth. They
>   Break our skin upon the ground, fearful
>   That we guard the wisdom of Earth,
>   Our Mother.
> FOREST HEAD: Have you a grievance?
> ANT LEADER: None Father, except great clods of earth
>   Pressed on our feet. The world is old
>   But the rust of a million years
>   Has left the chains unloosened.
> FOREST HEAD: Are you not free?
> ANT LEADER: Freedom we have
>   Like the hunter on a precipice
>   And the horns of a rhinoceros
>   Nuzzling his buttocks.

FOREST HEAD: Do you not walk? Talk? Bear
 And suckle children by the gross?
ANT LEADER: Freedom indeed we have
 To choose our path
 To turn to the left or the right
 Like the spider in the sand-pit
 And the great ball of eggs
 Pressing on his back.
FOREST HEAD: But who are you?
 [*The leader retreats, and another takes his place.*]
ANT: I thought, staying this low,
 They would ignore me. I am the one
 That tried to be forgotten.
ANOTHER: I am the victim of the careless stride.
ANOTHER: I know the path was thin, a trickle
 In the marsh. Yet we mowed the roots
 Our bellies to the ground.
FOREST HEAD: Have you a Cause, or shall I
 Preserve you like a riddle?
ANT LEADER: We are the ones remembered
 When nations build . . .
ANOTHER: . . . with tombstones.
ANOTHER: We are the dried leaves, impaled
 On one-eyed brooms.
ANOTHER: We are the headless bodies when
 The spade of progress delves.
ANOTHER: The ones that never looked up when
 The wind turned suddenly, erupting
 In our heads.
ANOTHER: Down the axis of the world, from
 The whirlwind to the frozen drifts,
 We are the ever legion of the world,
 Smitten, for—'the good to come'.

of the Forests

ANT LEADER: Once my eyes were earthworms
　　Dragging in my tears.
ARONI: [*shouting.*] What is this? For what cursed future
　　Do you rise to speak?
ANT LEADER: Then the ring of scourges was complete
　　And my hair rose on its tail
　　Like scorpions.
　　[*They vanish. The Figure in Red goes resolutely to Forest Head and confronts him. Forest Head appears hesitant, even reluctant. Eventually, he gestures brusquely to the Interpreter.*]
FOREST HEAD: Unmask them. The Half-Child has played out his game and lost. Let them see the rest with their natural eyes, their human sight.
　　[*The Interpreter unmasks all three. Enter the first of the Triplets. It is the lower trunk of a body, with arms. Loose, uncontrolled manner.*]
FIRST TRIPLET: [*speaking as he comes in.*] Has anyone found the Means? I am the End that will justify it.
　　[*The Interpreter turns quickly and does a round of 'ampe' with him. Enter second Triplet. An over-blown head, drooling.*]
SECOND TRIPLET: I am the Greater Cause, standing ever ready, excusing the crimes of today for tomorrow's mirage. Hungry I come, hearing there was a feast for the dead... Am I expected?
　　[*The Interpreter and the Second Triplet 'ampe', then the Interpreter with the First, and then the two Triplets together.*]
SECOND TRIPLET: [*stops suddenly. Goes to where Demoke, etc., stand huddled together. Sniffs them, turns them to the Interpreter.*] But who are these?
FOREST HEAD: They are the lesser criminals, pursuing the destructive path of survival. Weak, pitiable criminals, hiding their cowardice in sudden acts of bluster. And you obscenities...

[*Waves his hand towards the Triplets, who shriek and dance in delight.*] You perversions are born when they acquire power over one another, and their instincts are fulfilled a thousandfold, a hundred thousandfold. But wait, there is still the third triplet to come. You have as always, decided your own fates. Today is no different from your lives. I merely sit and watch.

[*Enter the Third Triplet, fanged and bloody.*]

THIRD TRIPLET: I find I am Posterity. Can no one see on what milk I have been nourished?

[*The Figure in Red rips off his head-cover. It is Eshuoro. Reaches a hand for the Half-child. Ogun steps forward.*]

OGUN: You fooled no one.

ESHUORO: Beware. I won him fairly.

OGUN: You play too many roles Eshuoro. Watch out for the mask that is lined with scorpions. [*Goes out.*]

[*Eshuoro again stretches a hand towards the Half-Child, who tries to go to the Dead Woman.*]

HALF-CHILD: I found an egg, smooth as a sea-pebble.

ESHUORO: [*gleefully.*] Took it home with him,
Warmed it in his bed of rushes
And in the night the egg was hatched
And the serpent came and swallowed him.

[*The Half-Child begins to spin round and round, till he is quite giddy. Stops suddenly.*]

HALF-CHILD: Still I fear the fated bearing
Still I circle yawning wombs.

DEAD WOMAN: Better not to know the bearing
Better not to bear the weaning
I who grow the branded navel
Shudder at the visitation
Shall my breast again be severed
Again and yet again be severed

of the Forests 81

> From its right of sanctity?
> Child, your hand is pure as sorrow
> Free me of the endless burden,
> Let this gourd, let this gourd
> Break beyond my hearth...

[*The Half-Child continues slowly towards the Mother, Eshuoro imperiously offering his hand, furious as each step takes the child nearer her. Looks up sharply and finds Ogun on the other side of the woman, with hand similarly outstretched. Snaps his fingers suddenly at the Interpreter. A clap of drums, and the Interpreter begins another round of 'ampe' with the Third Triplet. The Woman's hand and the Half-Child's are just about to meet when this happens, and the child turns instantly, attracted by the game. The 'ampe' gradually increases tempo among the three Triplets. The Interpreter throws off his mask, reveals himself as Eshuoro's Jester. He draws the child into a game of 'ampe'. When the Half-Child is totally disarmed by the Jester, Eshuoro picks him up suddenly and throws him towards the Third Triplet who makes to catch him on the point of two knives as in the dance of the child acrobats. Rola screams, the Child is tossed up by the Third Triplet who again goes through the same motion, the other two Triplets continuing the furious 'ampe' round him and yelling at the top of their voices. Demoke, Rola and Adenebi again cluster together. The Half-Child is now tossed back to Eshuoro, and suddenly Demoke dashes forward to intercept. Eshuoro laughs, pretends to throw the child back, Demoke dashes off only to find that he still retains the child. The Interpreter, Eshuoro and the Third Triplet all evading the knife-points at the last moment and catching the Half-Child in the crook of their elbows.*

They keep up this game for a brief period, with Demoke running between them, until Ogun appears behind the Interpreter, pulls him aside just as the child is thrown towards him, makes

*the catch himself passing it instantly to Demoke who has come
running as before.
All action stops again, including the first and second Triplets
who have never ceased to 'ampe'. They all look at Demoke,
who stands confused, not knowing what the next step should be.
He decides eventually to restore the child to the Dead Woman,
and attempts to do so. Eshuoro partially blocks his way and
appeals to Forest Head. Ogun appeals against him.*]

FOREST HEAD: [*more to himself.*] Trouble me no further. The
fooleries of beings whom I have fashioned closer to me
weary and distress me. Yet I must persist, knowing that
nothing is ever altered. My secret is my eternal burden—
to pierce the encrustations of soul-deadening habit, and bare
the mirror of original nakedness—knowing full well, it is
all futility. Yet I must do this alone, and no more, since to
intervene is to be guilty of contradiction, and yet to remain
altogether unfelt is to make my long-rumoured ineffectuality
complete; hoping that when I have tortured awareness
from their souls, that perhaps, only perhaps, in new
beginnings. . . . Aroni, does Demoke know the meaning
of his act?

ARONI: Demoke, you hold a doomed thing in your hand. It is no
light matter to reverse the deed that was begun many lives
ago. The Forest will not let you pass.

[*The Woman appeals, mutely to Demoke. All eyes are intent
upon Demoke until he makes up his mind; gives the child to the
Dead Woman. Immediately, Aroni leads out the Dead
Woman with the Half-Child. Forest Head takes a final
look at the gathering, goes off. Eshuoro gives a loud yell of
triumph, rushes off-stage, accompanied by his jester. The
Triplets follow gleefully.
A silhouette of Demoke's totem is seen. The village people
dancing round it, also in silhouette, in silence. There is no*

of the Forests

contact between them and the Forest ones. The former in fact are not aware of the other beings. Eshuoro's Jester leaps on stage, bearing the sacrificial basket which he clamps on to Demoke's head; performing a wild dance in front of him. Eshuoro re-enters, bearing a heavy club. **Dance of the Unwilling Sacrifice,** *in which Eshuoro and his Jester head Demoke relentlessly towards the totem and the silent dancing figures. Rola and Adenebi are made to sprinkle libation on the scene, continuously as in a trance. Demoke, headed towards his handiwork is faded away, and re-appears at the foot of the totem, the crowd parting in silence. He begins to climb, hampered further by the load on his head. There are only the drums, Eshuoro and his Jester have stopped dancing. Slowly, Demoke disappears from view, and the crowd cheer wildly, without sound. Eshuoro rushes out in a frenzy. Returns at the totem with a fire-brand; sets fire to the tree. Enter Ogun, catches Demoke as he falls. Black-out. Then the front gets increasingly lighter as Eshuoro returns and dances out his frenzy, lashing his Jester with a branch.*

Noise of the beaters from a distance. Dawn is breaking. Ogun enters bearing Demoke, eyeing the sky anxiously. He is armed with a gun and cutlass. The sun creeps through; Ogun gently lays down Demoke, leaves his weapons beside him, flees. Eshuoro is still dancing as the foremost of the beaters break on the scene and then he flees after his Jester.

It is now fully dawn. Agboreko and the Old Man enter, Murete, very drunk, dragging them on. The sound of the main body of beaters with the drummers continues in the distance.]

MURETE: Here, I said it was here.

AGBOREKO: I will not forget my promise.

[*The Old Man rushes towards Demoke, lying inert, raises him to a sitting position. Demoke opens his eyes.*]

OLD MAN: Safe! What did you see? What did you see?

AGBOREKO: Let them be, old man. When the crops have been gathered it will be time enough for the winnowing of the grains. Prov ...

MURETE: [*drunkenly.*] Proverbs to bones and silence.

AGBOREKO: It is time to think of the fulfilment of vows.

OLD MAN: [*to Demoke.*] We searched all night. Knowing who your companion was ...

AGBOREKO: Madame Tortoise ... the one who never dies ... never ...

OLD MAN: And then I was troubled by the mystery of the fourth. The council orator I knew. And Madame Tortoise. But the fourth ... [*he looks round.*] You are back to three. Did the other reveal himself?

DEMOKE: The father of ghommids. Forest Head himself.

AGBOREKO: At first we thought it would be Eshuoro, tricking you onwards like the echo in the woods. And then I thought, Murete cannot be silent only from fear. It must be Forest Head himself.

OLD MAN: Forest Head! And did you see the lame one?
[*Demoke nods.*]
Fools we were to pit our weakness against the cunning of Aroni, chasing souls whom he was resolved to welcome.

AGBOREKO: We paid dearly for this wisdom newly acquired.

OLD MAN: Cruelly. Look, look at me. Behind every sapling, there was the sudden hand of Aroni, and he aims well.
[*Gingerly feels a weal across his face.*]

DEMOKE: There was a path that brought us here. Could not Murete find it?

OLD MAN: We would have done better without him. Sometimes I suspect his drunkenness. We have tasted the night thickness of the forest like the nails of a jealous wife.
[*Agboreko nudges the Old Man. He becomes suddenly uncomfortable, hems and coughs.*]

of the Forests

OLD MAN: Demoke, we made sacrifice and demanded the path of expiation...

DEMOKE: Expiation? We three who lived many lives in this one night, have we not done enough? Have we not felt enough for the memory of our remaining lives?

OLD MAN: What manner of a night was it? Can you tell us that? In this wilderness, was there a kernel of light?
[Rola comes forward. She looks chastened.]

AGBOREKO: I did not think to find her still alive, this one who outlasts them all. Madame Tortoise...

DEMOKE: Not any more. It was the same lightning that seared us through the head.

AGBOREKO: [snorts.] Does that mean something wise, child? [Sneaking up to Demoke.] Of the future, did you learn anything?

OLD MAN: [comes up and pulls him away.] 'When the crops have been gathered...'

AGBOREKO: [reproved. With ponderous finality.] Proverb to bones and silence.
[A brief silence.]
[Then, spoken in a sense of epilogue, Igbale music gently in the background.]

DEMOKE: Darkness enveloped me, but piercing
    Through I came
Night is the choice for the fox's dance.
Child of the Moon's household am I.

AGBOREKO: I made a sponge of nettle pods.
The crocodile scratching taught me then
My veins run with the oil of palms.

OLD MAN: The glare of the Lion turned him blind.
The enemy's death-blow broke his arm.
Ruler of the Forest depths am I.

ROLA: Witches spread their net, trapped emptiness

Does the tear in the wind's eye pause to dry?
Palm of the storm's hand am I.
ADENEBI: When the rock fell, alone I caught the boulders.
My saddle is the torrent of the flood.
Serpent of the ocean depths am I.
DEMOKE: And the lightning made his bid—in vain
When she cooks, is the cloud ever set on fire?
I lodge below, with the secrets of Earth.
[*Up Igbale drums, strongly.*]

THE END

The 'Dance for the Half-Child' as it was performed in the 1960 production

DEAD WOMAN: Better not to know the bearing
    Better not to bear the weaning
    I who grow the branded navel
    Shudder at the visitation
    Shall my breast again be severed
    Again and yet again be severed
    From its right and sanctity?
    Child, your hand is pure as sorrow
    Free me of the endless burden,
    Let this gourd, let this gourd
    Break beyond my hearth...

[*The Half-Child continues slowly towards the Mother, Eshuoro imperiously offering his hand, furious as each step takes the child nearer her. Looks up sharply and finds Ogun on the other side of the woman, with hand similarly outstretched. Snaps his fingers suddenly at the Interpreter. A clap of drums, and the Interpreter begins another round of* ampe *with the Third Triplet. The Woman's hand and the Half-Child's are just about to meet when this happens, and the child turns instantly, attracted by the game. Hanging carelessly from the hand of the Half-Child is the wood figure of an* ibeji *which he has clutched from his first appearance. Eshuoro waits until he is totally mesmerized by the Jester's antics, snatches it off him and throws it to the Third Triplet. It jerks the Half-Child awake and he runs after it. Third Triplet, the Interpreter and Eshuoro toss the* ibeji *to one another while the child runs between them trying to recover it, but they only taunt him with it and throw it over his head. The*

First and Second Triplets keep up their incessant ampe. *The Interpreter is standing near Demoke, and suddenly he pulls the Interpreter aside, catches the* ibeji. *Eshuoro moves at once to the Half-Child but he runs to Demoke and clings to him. Everything stops. Eshuoro silently appeals to Forest Head, Ogun appeals against him.*

FOREST HEAD: [*more to himself.*] Trouble me no further. The fooleries of beings whom I have fashioned closer to me weary and distress me. Yet I must persist, knowing that nothing is ever altered. My secret is my eternal burden—to pierce the encrustations of soul-deadening habit, and bare the mirror of original nakedness—knowing full well, it is all futility. Yet I must do this alone, and no more, since to intervene is to be guilty of contradiction, and yet to remain altogether unfelt is to make my long-rumoured ineffectuality complete; hoping that when I have tortured awareness from their souls, that perhaps, only perhaps, in new beginnings ... Aroni, does Demoke know the meaning of his act?

[*Exit Forest Head, displaying a long-suffering irritation.*]

ARONI: Demoke, you hold a doomed thing in your hand. It is no light matter to reverse the deed that was begun many lives ago. The Forest will not let you pass.

[*The Dead Woman appeals, mutely to Demoke. All eyes are intent on Demoke until he makes up his mind. Restores the 'ibeji' to the Half-Child. Again Eshuoro turns to Forest Head but he is no longer there. He looks to Aroni for interference but Aroni refuses to notice any more, sits down where Forest Head sat earlier. The Interpreter signals urgently off-stage, and immediately a group of forest creatures enter, all replicas of the Jester, do an* atilogwu-*ordered dance towards the Half-Child. Ogun snatches a cutlass, Eshuoro a Club, and they clash briefly, across the dancers. As the jesters stamp towards the Half-Child again, Demoke picks him up and seats him on one shoulder, tries to move towards the Dead Woman standing with eager arms outstretched. They manoeuvre Demoke away at every attempt he makes. On one side Eshuoro swinging his club, prowling, trembling from head to foot in elemental fury. Ogun on the other, watchful, cutlass at the ready. Both are kept apart by the dancers only, and from time to time they clash, always briefly, and they spring apart again.*

It begins to lighten. In the distance, faint sounds of the beaters come over the music of the forest drums. Demoke gets wearier and wearier, begins to sag. At every falter the Jesters move towards him to snatch their quarry but he recovers.

The scene brightens. The Triplets scatter. Aroni looks at the sky, slips off. Ogun and Eshuoro lose control, fly at each other, seemingly blind. They miss, begin to feel for the other's position, flailing wildly. Coming suddenly on each other, they lock together, bear each other out of sight.

The Forest rhythm becomes thoroughly confused with the beaters' music and shortly after, the Jesters stop totally, bewildered. The First Jester looks at the sky, flees, and they follow. Demoke sags to his knees, the Dead Woman runs to him, snatches the falling Half-Child and is swallowed by the forest. Demoke collapses on the ground.

It is now fully dawn.

Entry of Agboreko and the Old Man, led by Murete.]

—al Fin.